COLLINS GEM

Dutch
PHRASE FINDER

HarperCollins*Publishers*

CONSULTANT
Ben Braber Ph.D.

First published 1994
Copyright © HarperCollins Publishers
Reprint 10 9 8 7 6 5 4
Printed and bound in Great Britain by
Caledonian International Book Manufacturing Ltd,
Glasgow G64 2QT

ISBN 0 00-470686-2

Your *Collins Gem Phrase Finder* is designed to help you locate the exact phrase you need in any situation, whether for holiday or business. If you want to adapt the phrases, we have made sure that you can easily see where to substitute your own words (you can find them in the dictionary section), and the clear, alphabetical, two-colour layout gives you direct access to the different topics.

The *Phrase Finder* includes:

■ Over 70 topics arranged alphabetically from **ACCOMMODATION** to **WORK**. Each phrase is accompanied by a simple pronunciation guide which ensures that there's no problem over pronouncing the foreign words.

■ Practical hints and useful vocabulary highlighted in boxes. Where the English words appear first in the box, this indicates vocabulary you may need. Where the red Dutch words appear first, these are words you are more likely to see written on signs and notices.

WORDS APPEARING IN BLACK ARE ENGLISH WORDS	WORDS APPEARING IN RED ARE DUTCH WORDS

■ Possible phrases you may hear in reply to your questions. The foreign phrases appear in red.

■ A clearly laid-out 5000-word dictionary: English words appear in black and Dutch words appear in red.

■ A basic grammar section which will enable you to build on your phrases.

It's worth spending time before you embark on your travels just looking through the topics to see what is covered and becoming familiar with what might be said to you.

Whatever the situation, your *Phrase Finder* is sure to help!

CONTENTS

LIST OF TOPICS

*The syllable to be stressed is marked in **heavy italics**.*

b, d, f, h, l, m, n, ng (combination), s, z like English

d at the end of a word usually sounds like t

*n in words ending -en is often not pronounced properly, with the e which preceeds that n to sound like u (as in **hurt**)*

k, p, t like English but not aspirated

r like English but more rolled

v like English but more aspirated

w like English v but less aspirated

Dutch vowels can have short and long sounds.

DUTCH	SOUNDS LIKE	EXAMPLE	PRONUNCIATION
a	sm**a**rt	mast	mast
a/aa	**ah**	straten/maat	**strah**-tu/maht
e	b**e**st	best	best
e	h**u**rt	de	du
e/ee	m**ay**	negen/see	**nay**-CHu/zay
i	**i**t	witte	**wit**-tu
ie	f**ee**t	niet	neet
o	sh**o**rt	kort	kort
o/oo	**oh**	mooi/boot	mohee/boht
oe	f**oo**t	moet	moot
ou/au	h**ou**se	mouw/nauw	mouw/nouw
u	h**u**rt	kunt	kunt
u/uu	**yuh**	uw	uuw
ei/ij	*ei – no equivalent in English, try **e** and **ay** in rapid successsion*		
eu	*eu – no equivalent in English, try **ay** through the nose with rounded lips pointing forward.*		
ui	*ui – no equivalent in English, try **e** and **i** in rapid succession with mouth open wide and more aspirated.*		
g/ch	lo**ch**	mag/tochten	maCH/**toCHt**-u
j	**y**es	ja	yah
sj	**sh**ort	meisje	**mei**-shu
tj	**ch**at	diertje	**deer**-chu
sch	*sch – no equivalent in English, try **s** and **CH** in rapid succession.*		

6

KAMERS VRIJ	ROOMS AVAILABLE
VOL	FULL UP
PENSION	GUEST HOUSE

Do you have a list of accommodation with prices?
Heeft u een lijst met hotels en pensions met prijzen?

*hayft uu un leist met hoh-**tels** en **pen**-shons met **prei**-zu*

Is there a hotel here?
Is er hier een hotel?

*is er heer un hoh-**tel***

Do you have any vacancies?
Heeft u een kamer vrij?

*hayft uu un **kah**-mur vrei*

Do I have to book?
Moet ik reserveren?

*moot ik ray-sur-**vay**-ru*

I'd like a room...
Ik wil een kamer...

*ik wil un **kah**-mur...*

double
tweepersoons

***tway**-per-sohns*

single
eenpersoons

***ayn**-per-sohns*

with bath
met een bad

met un bad

with shower
met een douche

met un doosh

with a double bed
met een tweepersoonsbed

*met un **tway**-per-sohns-bed*

twin-bedded
met twee bedden

*met tway **bed**du*

with an extra bed for a child
met een extra bed voor een kind

met un extrah bed vohr un kind

A room that looks...
Een kamer die uitkijkt...

*un **kah**-mur dee uitkeikt...*

onto the garden
op de tuin

op du tuin

onto the sea
op de zee

op du zay

We'd like two rooms next to each other
Wij willen twee kamers naast elkaar

*wei **wil**-lu tway **kah**-murs nahst elkahr*

CONT.

7

We'll stay ... nights
Wij blijven ... nachten
*wei **blei**-vu ... na**CH**-tu*

from ... till...
van ... tot...
van ... tot...

I will confirm...
Ik zal bevestigen...
*ik zal bu-**ves**-ti-CHu...*

by letter
per brief
per breef

by fax
per fax
per fax

How much is it...?
Hoeveel is het...?
hoo-vayl is het...

per night
per nacht
*per na**CH**t*

per week
per week
per wayk

Is dinner included?
Is het diner inbegrepen?
*is het dee-**nay** in-bu-**CH**ray-pu*

Have you anything cheaper?
Heeft u iets goedkopers?
*hayft uu eets **CH**ood-koh-pers*

Only bed and breakfast
Alleen een kamer met ontbijt
*al-**layn** un **kah**-mur met ont-beit*

Can you suggest somewhere else?
Kunt u iets anders suggereren?
*kunt uu eets **an**-ders suCH-CHU-**ray**-ru*

■ **YOU MAY HEAR**

We zijn vol
wu zein vol
We're full up

Voor hoeveel nachten?
*vohr **hoo**-vayl **naCH**-tu*
For how many nights?

Uw naam, alstublieft
*uuw nahm als-tuu-**bleeft***
Your name, please?

Bevestig alstublieft...
*bu-**ves**-TiCH als-tuu-**bleeft**...*
Please confirm...

per brief
per breef
by letter

per fax
per fax
by fax

■ **CAMPING** ■ **HOTEL** ■ **SIGHTSEEING & TOURIST OFFICE**

AMOUNT (of money)	BEDRAG, HET
DELIVERY	LEVERING, DE
INVOICE	REKENING, DE / FACTUUR, DE
ORDER	BESTELLING, DE

I'd like to speak to someone in your accounts department
Ik wil spreken met iemand van uw administratie
*ik wil **spray**-ku met **ee**-mand van uuw ad-mee-**nee**-strah-tsee*

It's regarding invoice number...
Het betreft rekeningnummer...
*het bu-**treft** **ray**-ku-ning-num-mer...*

I think that there is an error
Ik denk dat er een fout is
ik denk dat er un fout is

We are still waiting for the invoice to be settled
Wij wachten nog op betaling van de rekening
*wei **waCH**-tu noCH op bu-**tah**-ling van de **ray**-ku-ning*

Please send a credit note and new invoice
Alstublieft, stuur een creditnota en een nieuwe rekening
*als-tuu-**bleeft** stuur un **cray**-dit-noh-tah en un **nee**-we **ray**-ku-ning*

Please address the invoice to...
Alstublieft adresseer de rekening aan...
*als-tuu-**bleeft** ah-dres-sayr du **ray**-ku-ning ahn...*

The goods should be accompanied by an invoice
De goederen moeten vergezeld zijn van een factuur
*du **goo**-du-ru **moo**-tu ver-CHu-**zelt** zein van un fak-**tuur***

Please state content and value of the consignment
Alstublieft, beschrijf inhoud en waarde van de zending
*als-tuu-**bleeft** bu-**schreif** in-**houd** en **wahr**-de van de **zen**-ding*

■ **NUMBERS** ■ **TELEPHONE**

Most signs are in Dutch and English and you may go through the airport without having to speak any Dutch. Here are a few signs you will find useful to know.

AANKOMST	ARRIVALS
PASPOORTCONTROLE	PASSPORT CONTROL
EU PASPOORTHOUDERS	EU PASSPORT HOLDERS
BAGAGE	BAGGAGE RECLAIM
DOUANE	CUSTOMS CONTROL
NIETS AAN TE GEVEN	NOTHING TO DECLARE
AANGIFTE GOEDEREN	ARTICLES TO DECLARE
BABYVERZORGING	BABYROOM
UITGANG	EXIT
TOILETTEN	TOILETS
ONTMOETINGSPUNT	MEETING POINT

Where is the luggage for the flight from...?
Waar is de bagage van de vlucht uit...?

*wahr is du bah-**CHah**-shu van du vluCHt uit...*

Where can I change some money?
Waar kan ik geld wisselen?

*wahr kan ik CHeld **wis**-su-lu*

How do I get to the centre of *(name town)***...?**
Hoe kom ik in het centrum van...?

*hoo kom ik in het **cen**-trum van...*

How much is a taxi...?	**into town**	**to the hotel**
hoeveel is een taxi...?	naar de stad	naar het hotel
*hoo-vayl is un tak-**see**...*	*nahr du stad*	*nahr het hoh-**tel***

Is there a bus or train to the city centre?
Is er een bus of trein naar het centrum?

*is er un bus of trein nahr het **cen**-trum*

■ BUS ■ LUGGAGE ■ METRO ■ TAXI

VERTREK	**DEPARTURES**
INSTAPKAART	**BOARDING CARD**
UITGANG	**BOARDING GATE**
CHECK-IN	**CHECK IN**
VLUCHT	**FLIGHT**
VERTRAGING	**DELAY**

Where do I check in for the flight to...?
Waar moet ik inchecken voor de vlucht naar...?
*whar moot ik in-**check**-u vohr du vluCHt nahr...*

Which is the departure gate for the flight to...?
Waar is de uitgang voor de vlucht naar...?
*wahr is de **uit**-CHang vohr du vluCHt nahr...*

■ YOU MAY HEAR

Laatste oproep voor passagiers voor vlucht...
*laht-stu **op**-roop vohr pass-**sah**-sheers vohr vluCHt...*
Last call for passengers on flight...

Uw vlucht is vertraagd
*uuw vluCHt is ver-**trahCHd***
Your flight is delayed

■ IF YOU NEED TO CHANGE OR CHECK ON YOUR FLIGHT

I want to change / cancel my reservation
Ik wil mijn reservering veranderen / annuleren
*ik wil mein ray-ser-**vay**-ring ver-**an**-du-ru / an-nuu-**lay**-ry*

I'd like to reconfirm my flight to...
Ik wil mijn vlucht naar ... bevestigen
*ik wil mein vluCHt nahr ... bu-**ves**-ti-CHu*

Is the flight to ... delayed?
Is de vlucht naar ... vertraagd?
*is de vluCHt nahr ... ver-**trahCHd***

11

The Dutch alphabet is the same as the English. Below are letters used for clarification when spelling something out.

How do you spell it?
  Hoe spel je het?

hoo spel yu het

A as in Amsterdam, b as in Bravo
A van Amsterdam, b van bravo

*ah van am-ster-**dam**, bay van **brah**-voh*

A	ah	**Amsterdam**	am-ster-**dam**
B	bay	**Bravo**	**brah**-voh
C	cay	**Charlie**	char-**lee**
D	day	**Dirk**	dirk
E	ay	**Edam**	**ay**-dam
F	ef	**Freddie**	fre-**dee**
G	CHay	**goed**	CHood
H	hah	**help**	help
I	ee	**Isaac**	**ee**-sahk
J	yay	**Jaap**	yahp
K	kah	**kilo**	**kee**-loh
L	el	**lasso**	las-**soh**
M	em	**moeder**	**moo**-der
N	en	**Nico**	**nee**-ko
O	oh	**Otto**	ot-**toh**
P	pay	**paard**	pahrd
Q	kuu	**Quaker**	**kway**-ker
R	er	**Rudolf**	**ruu**-dolf
S	es	**suiker**	**sui**-ker
T	tay	**tafel**	**tah**-fel
U	uu	**uur**	uur
V	vay	**vogel**	**voh**-CHel
W	way	**wind**	wind
X	iks	**xylofoon**	see-loh-**phohn**
Y	ei	**Yankee**	**yan**-kee
Z	zet	**zout**	zout

Yes
Ja
yah

No
Nee
nay

OK!
O.K.
*o-**kay***

Please
Alstublieft
*als-tuu-**bleeft***

Don't mention it
Graag gedaan
*CHrahCH CHu-**dahn***

With pleasure!
Graag
CHrahCH

Thank you
Dank u
dank uu

Thanks very much
Dank u wel
dank uu wel

That's very kind
Dat is erg aardig
*dat is erCH **ahr**-diCH*

Sir / Mr
Meneer
*mu-**nayr***

Madam / Mrs / Ms
Mevrouw
*mu-**vrouw***

Miss
Mejuffrouw
*mu-**yuf**-frouw*

Excuse me! *(to catch attention)*
Pardon!
*par-**don***

Excuse me *(sorry)*
Het spijt me
het speit mu

Pardon?
Pardon?
*par-**don***

I don't know
Ik weet het niet
ik wayt het neet

I don't understand
Ik begrijp het niet
*ik bu-**CHreip** het neet*

Do you understand?
Begrijp u het?
*bu-**CHreipt** uu het*

Do you speak English?
Spreekt u Engels?
*spraykt uu **eng**-els*

I speak very little Dutch
Ik spreek weinig Nederlands
*ik sprayk wei-niCH **nay**-der-lands*

Could you repeat that, please?
Kunt u dat herhalen, alstublieft?
*kunt uu dat her-**hah**-lu als-tuu-**bleeft***

May I...?
Mag ik...?
maCH ik...

It doesn't matter
Het geeft niet
het gayft neet

I would like...
Ik zou graag...
ik zou ChrahCH...

Do you have...?
Heeft u...?
hayft uu...

CROSSING	OVERSTEEK, DE
CRUISE	CRUISE, DE
CABIN	CABINE, DE

When is the next boat / ferry to...?
Wanneer vertrekt de volgende boot / veerboot naar...?
*wan-nayr ver-**trekt** du **vol**-CHen-du boht / **vayr**-boht nahr...*

Have you a timetable?
Heeft u een dienstregeling?
*hayft uu un **deenst**-ray-CHu-ling*

Is there a car ferry to...?
Is er een autoveer naar...?
*is er un **ou**-toh-vayr nahr...*

How much is the ticket...?
Hoeveel is een kaartje...?
*hoo-vayl is un **kahr**-chu...*

single	return
enkel	retour
en-kel	ru-**toor**

A day return
Een dagretour
*un daCH-ru-**toor***

How much is the crossing for a car and ... people?
Hoeveel is de oversteek voor een auto en ... personen?
*hoo-vayl is du **oh**-ver-stayk vohr un **ou**-toh en ... per-**soh**-nu*

How long is the journey?
Hoelang duurt de reis?
hoo-lang duurt du reis

What time do we get to...?
Hoe laat komen we aan in...?
*hoo laht **koh**-mu wu ahn in...*

Where does the boat leave?
Waar vertrekt de boot?
*wahr ver-**trekt** du boht*

When is the first / last boat?
Hoe laat is de eerste / laatste boot?
*hoo laht is du **ayr**-stu / **laht**-stu boht*

Is there a restaurant / snack bar on board?
Is er een restaurant / snackbar aan boord?
*is er un res-tou-**rant** / **snack**-bar ahn bohrd*

In Dutch it is possible to say:
I have a headache – ik heb hoofdpijn or
my head hurts – mijn hoofd doet pijn

ankle	enkel, de	**en**-kel
arm	arm, de	arm
back	rug, de	ruCH
bone	been, het / bot, het	bayn / bot
chin	kin, de	kin
ear	oor, het	ohr
elbow	elleboog, de	**el**-lu-bohCH
eye	oog, het	ohCH
finger	vinger, de	**ving**-er
foot	voet, de	voot
hair	haar, het	hahr
hand	hand, de	hand
head	hoofd, het	hohfd
heart	hart, het	hart
hip	heup, de	heup
joint	gewricht, het	CHu-**wriCHt**
kidney	nier, de	neer
knee	knie, de	knee
leg	been, het	bayn
liver	lever, de	**lay**-ver
mouth	mond, de	mond
nail	nagel, de	**nah**-CHel
neck	nek, de	nek
nose	neus, de	neus
stomach	maag, de / buik, de	mahCH / buik
throat	keel, de	kayl
thumb	duim, de	duim
toe	teen, de	tayn
wrist	pols, de	pols

■ DOCTOR ■ PHARMACY

15

Can you help me?
Kunt u me helpen?
*kunt u mu **hel**-pu*

My car has broken down
Mijn auto is kapot
*mein **ou**-toh is **kah**-pot*

The car won't start
De auto wil niet starten
*du **ou**-toh wil neet **star**-tu*

Can you give me a push?
Kunt u mij duwen?
*kunt uu mei **duu**-wu*

I've run out of petrol
Ik heb geen benzine meer
*ik heb gayn ben-**zee**-nu mayr*

Is there a garage near here?
Is er een garage in de buurt?
*is er un CHah-**rah**-shu in de buurt*

The engine is overheating
De motor is oververhit
*du **moh**-ter is **oh**-ver-ver-hit*

The battery is flat
De accu is leeg
*du **ak**-kuu is layCH*

I need water
Ik heb water nodig
*ik heb **wah**-ter **noh**-diCH*

The petrol / oil is leaking
De benzine / olie lekt
*du ben-**zee**-nu / **oh**-lee lekt*

I've a flat tyre
Ik heb een lekke band
*ik heb un **lek**-ku band*

I can't get the wheel off
Ik krijg het wiel er niet af
ik kreiCH het weel er neet af

Can you tow me to the nearest garage?
Kunt u mij naar de dichtstbijzijnste garage slepen?
*kunt uu mei nahr du **diCHt**st-bei-zein-ste CHa-**rah**-shu **slay**-pu*

Do you have parts for a (make of car)**...?**
Heeft u onderdelen voor...?
*hayft uu **on**-der-day-lu vohr...*

The ... doesn't work properly (see **CAR–PARTS**)
De / Het ... werkt niet goed
du / het ... werkt neet CHood

Can you replace the windscreen?
Kunt u mijn voorruit vervangen?
*kunt uu mein **vohr**-ruit ver-**vang**-u*

■ CAR – PARTS

16

For local Dutch public transport you need to buy multiple-journey cards (10 or more journeys) called **strippenkaarten**.

Is there a bus to...?
Is er een bus naar...?
is er un bus nahr...

Which bus goes to...?
Welke bus gaat naar...?
***wel**-ku bus CHaht nahr...*

Where do I catch the bus to...?
Waar neem ik de bus naar...?
wahr naym ik du bus nahr...

We're going to...
We gaan naar...
wu CHahn nahr...

Where do they sell strippenkaarten?
Waar verkopen ze strippenkaarten?
*wahr ver-**koh**-pu zu **strip**-pu-kahr-tu*

How much is it to...?
Hoeveel is het naar...?
***hoo**-vayl is het nahr...*

the centre	**the beach**	**the airport**	**Amsterdam**
het centrum	het strand	het vliegveld	Amsterdam
*het **cen**-trum*	*het strand*	*het **vleeCH**-veld*	*am-ster-**dam***

How often are the buses to...?
Hoe vaak gaan er bussen naar...?
*hoo vahk CHahn er **bus**-su nahr...*

When is the first / last bus to...?
Hoe laat gaat de eerste / laatste bus naar...?
*hoo laht CHaht du **ayr**-stu / **laht**-stu bus nahr...*

Tell me when I must get off, please
Zeg me wanneer ik moet uitstappen, alstublieft
*zeCH mu wan-**nayr** ik moot **uit**-stap-pu als-tuu-**bleeft***

I want to get off, please
Ik wil uitstappen, alstublieft
*ik wil **uit**-stap-pu als-tuu-**bleeft***

This is my stop
Dit is mijn halte
*dit is mein **hal**-tu*

■ **YOU MAY HEAR**

De bus stopt niet in...
du bus stopt neet in...
This bus doesn't stop in...

U moet de ... nemen
*uu moot du ... **nay**-mu*
You have to catch the...

■ **METRO** ■ **TAXI**

BOARD MEETING	DIRECTIEVERGADERING, DE
CONFERENCE ROOM	CONFERENTIEZAAL, DE
MANAGING DIRECTOR	DIRECTEUR, DE
MEETING	VERGADERING, DE
MINUTES	NOTULEN, DE
SAMPLE	MONSTER, HET
TO CHAIR A MEETING	VOORZITTEN
TO DRAW UP A CONTRACT	EEN CONTRACT OPMAKEN
TRADE FAIR	HANDELSBEURS, DE
TURNOVER	OMZET, DE

I'd like to arrange a meeting with...
Ik wil graag een vergadering beleggen met...
ik wil CHrahCH un ver-CHah-du-ring bu-leCH-Chu met...

Are you free...?   on the 4th of May at 1100 am
Bent u vrij...?   op 4 mei om 11.00 uur
bent uu vrei...   *op veer mei om elf uur*

for meeting over...   lunch   dinner
voor een bespreking tijdens...   lunch   diner
vohr un bu-spray-king tei-dens...   *lunch*   *dee-nay*

I will confirm that...   by letter   by fax
Ik zal dat bevestigen...   per brief   per fax
ik zal dat bu-ves-ti-CHu...   *per breef*   *per fax*

I'm staying at Hotel...   How do I get to your office?
Ik logeer in hotel...   Hoe kom ik bij uw kantoor?
ik loh-shayr in hoh-tel...   *hoo kom ik bei uuw kan-tohr*

Let ... know that I will be ... minutes late, please
Laat ... weten dat ik ... minuten te laat ben, alstublieft
laht ... way-tu dat ik ... mee-nuu-tu tu laht ben als-tuu-bleeft

I have an appointment with...   at ... o'clock
Ik heb een afspraak met...   om ... uur
ik heb un af-sprahk met...   *om .. uur*

Here is my card
Hier is mijn visitekaartje
*heer is mein vee-**see**-tu-kahr-chu*

I'm delighted to meet you at last
Het doet mij een groot plezier u eindelijk te ontmoeten
*het doot mei un CHroht plu-**zeer** uu **ein**-du-luk tu ont-**moo**-tu*

I don't know much Dutch
Ik spreek niet veel Nederlands
*ik sprayk neet vayl **nay**-der-lands*

Can you speak more slowly?
Kunt u langzamer spreken?
*kunt uu **lang**-zah-mer **spray**-ku*

I'm sorry I'm late
Het spijt me dat ik te laat ben
het speit mu dat ik tu laht ben

My plane was delayed
Mijn vliegtuig had vertraging
*mein **vleeCH**-tuiCH had ver-**trah**-Ching*

May I introduce you to…
Mag ik u voorstellen aan…
*maCH ik u **vohr**-stel-lu ahn…*

Can I invite you to dinner?
Mag ik u uitnodigen voor het diner?
*maCH ik uu **uit**-noh-di-Chu vohr het dee-**nay***

■ YOU MAY HEAR

Heeft u een afspraak?
*hayft uu un af-**sprahk***
Do you have an appointment?

Meneer / Mevrouw … is niet op kantoor
*mu-**nayr** / mu-**vrouw** … is neet op kan-**tohr***
Mr / Mrs /Ms … isn't in the office

Hij / Zij komt over vijf minuten terug
*hei / zei komt **oh**-ver veif mee-**nuu**-tu tu-**rug***
He / She will be back in five minutes

■ FAX ■ LETTERS ■ OFFICE ■ TELEPHONE

*Local tourist offices have information on **campings**.*

Do you have a list of campsites with prices?
Heeft u een lijst van campings met prijzen?
*hayft uu un leist met **kem**-pings met **prei**-zu*

How far is...?	**the beach**	**the wood**
Hoe ver is...?	het strand	het bos
hoo ver is...	*het strand*	*het bos*

Is there a restaurant on the campsite?
Is er een restaurant op de camping?
*is er un res-tou-**rant** op du **kem**-ping*

Do you have any vacancies?
Zijn er vrije staanplaatsen?
*zein er **vrei**-u **stahn**-plaaht-su*

Are there showers?	**Is there hot water / electricity?**
Zijn er douches?	Is er warm water / elektriciteit?
*zein er **doo**-shes*	*is er warm **wah**-ter / ay-leck-tree-cee-**teit***

Is this included in the price?
Is dit inbegrepen in de prijs?
*is dit in-bu-**gray**-pu in de preis*

We'd like to stay for ... nights
Wij willen ... nachten blijven
*wei **wil**-lu ... **naCH**-tu **blei**-vu*

How much is it per night...?	**for a tent**	**per person**
Hoeveel is het per nacht...?	voor een tent	per persoon
***hoo**-vayl is het per naCHt...*	*vohr un tent*	*per per-**sohn***

Can we camp here overnight? *(for tent)*
Kunnen we hier vannacht kamperen?
*kun-nu we heer van-**naCHt** kem-**pay**-ru*

■ SIGHTSEEING & TOURIST OFFICE

PARKEREN	PARKING
AUTOWEG	MOTORWAY *(signs are in blue)*
GEEF VOORRANG	GIVE WAY
CENTRUM	CITY CENTRE
WEG AFGESLOTEN	ROAD CLOSED
RECHTS HOUDEN	KEEP RIGHT
RONDWEG	BYPASS
GEVAARLIJKE BOCHT	DANGEROUS BEND
EENRICHTINGSVERKEER	ONE-WAY STREET
LANGZAAM RIJDEN	SLOW DOWN
TOL	TOLL
NIET PARKEREN	NO PARKING
ZWARE VOERTUIGEN	HEAVY VEHICLES
SNELHEIDSLIMIET	SPEED LIMIT

Can I park here?
Kan ik hier parkeren?
kan ik heer par-__kay__-ru

Do I have to pay?
Moet ik betalen?
moot ik bu-__tah__-lu

We're going to...
Wij gaan naar...
wei CHahn nahr...

Is the motorway busy?
Is de autoweg druk?
is du __ou__-toh-weCH druk

How long for?
Hoelang?
hoo-lang

What is the best route?
Wat is de beste route?
wat is du __bes__-tu __roo__-tu

What is the best time to drive?
Wat is de beste tijd om te rijden?
wat is de __bes__-tu teid om tu __rei__-du

■ **BREAKDOWNS** ■ **PETROL STATION**

DRIVING LICENCE	RIJBEWIJS, HET
FULLY COMPREHENSIVE INSURANCE	ALL-IN VERZEKERING, DE
REVERSE GEAR	ACHTERUIT-VERSNELLING, DE

I want to hire a car   **for ... days**   **for the weekend**
Ik wil een auto huren   voor ... dagen   voor het weekeinde
*ik wil un **ou**-toh **huu**-ru*   *vohr ... **dah**-CHu*   *vohr het **wayk**-ein-du*

How much is it...?   **per day**   **per week**
Hoeveel is het...?   per dag   per week
***hoo**-vayl is het...*   *per daCH*   *per wayk*

How much is the deposit?
Hoeveel is de waarborgsom?
***hoo**-vayl is du **wahr**-borCH-som*

Is there a mileage (kilometre) charge?   **How much?**
Is er een kilometertoeslag?   Hoeveel?
*is er un **kee**-loh-may-ter-too-slaCH*   ***hoo**-vayl*

Is fully comprehensive insurance included in the price?
Is een all-in verzekering inbegrepen in de prijs?
*is un all-in ver-**zay**-ku-ring in-bu-**gray**-pu in du preis*

Do I have to return the car here?   **By what time?**
Moet ik de auto hier terugbrengen?   Hoe laat?
*moot ik du **ou**-toh heer tu-**ruCH**-breng-u*   *hoo laht*

I'd like to leave the car in...
Ik wil de auto laten staan in...
*ik wil du **ou**-toh **lah**-tu stahn in...*

Can you show me how the controls work?
Kunt u me laten zien hoe de besturing werkt?
*kunt uu mu **lah**-tu zeen hoo du bu-**stuu**-ring werkt*

■ **YOU MAY HEAR**

Breng de auto met een volle tank terug, alstublieft
*breng du **ou**-toh met un **vol**-lu tank tu-**ruCH** als-tuu-**bleeft***
Return the car with a full tank, please

The ... doesn't work	**The ... don't work**
De/het ... werkt niet	De ... werken niet
du/het ... werkt neet	*de ... **wer**-ku neet*

accelerator	gaspedaal, het	*CHas-pu-dahl*
battery	accu, de	*ak-kuu*
bonnet	motorkap, de	*moh-tor-kap*
brakes	remmen, de	*rem-mu*
choke	choke, de	*shohk*
clutch	koppeling, de	*kop-pu-ling*
distributor	verdeler, de	*ver-day-ler*
engine	motor, de	*moh-tor*
exhaust pipe	uitlaat, de	*uit-laht*
fuse	zekering, de	*zay-ku-ring*
gears	versnellingen, de	*ver-snel-ling-u*
handbrake	handrem, de	*hand-rem*
headlights	koplampen, de	*kop-lamp-u*
ignition	ontsteking, de	*ont-stay-king*
indicator	richtingaanwijzer, de	*riCH-ting-ahn-wei-zer*
points	contact, het	*kon-takt*
radiator	radiator, de	*rah-dee-ah-tor*
rear lights	achterlichten, de	*aCH-ter-liCH-tu*
seat belt	autogordel, de	*ou-toh-CHor-del*
spare wheel	reservewiel, het	*ru-ser-vu-weel*
spark plugs	bougie, de	*boo-shee*
steering	stuurinrichting, de	*stuur-in-viCH-ting*
steering wheel	stuurwiel, het	*stuur-weel*
tyre	band, de	*band*
wheel	wiel, het	*weel*
windscreen	voorruit, de	*vohr-ruit*
-- wiper	ruitenwisser, de	*rui-tu-wis-ser*

■ BREAKDOWNS ■ PETROL STATION

I wish you a...
Ik wens u...
ik wens uu...

I wish you a... *(familiar)*
Ik wens je...
ik wens yu...

Merry Christmas!
Vrolijk Kerstfeest!
vroh-luk kerst-fayst

Happy New Year!
Gelukkig Nieuwjaar!
gu-luk-kiCH neew-jahr

Happy birthday!
Prettige verjaardag!
pret-ti-CHu ver-jahr-daCH

A good trip!
Een goede reis!
un CHoo-du reis

Best wishes!
De beste wensen!
du bes-tu wen-su

Welcome!
Welkom!
wel-kom

Enjoy your meal!
Eet smakelijk!
ayt smah-ku-luk

Thanks, and you too!
Dank u,u ook!
dank uu uu ohk

Cheers!
Proost!
prohst

Congratulations! *(having a baby, getting married, etc.)*
Gefeliciteerd!
CHe-fay-li-ci-tayrd

■ **LETTERS** ■ **MAKING FRIENDS**

Foreign films in Dutch cinemas are usually subtitled.

VOOR PERSONEN BOVEN 18 JAAR	FOR PERSONS OVER 18
VOORSTELLING	PERFORMANCE

Where is the cinema?
Waar is de bioscoop?
*wahr is du bee-os-**kohp***

When does (name film) **start?**
Hoe laat begint...?
*hoo laht bu-**CHint**...*

How much are the tickets?
Hoeveel zijn de kaartjes?
***hoo**-vayl zein du **kahr**-chus*

Two for the showing at... *(tirne)*
Twee voor de voorstelling van...
*tway vohr du **vohr**-stel-ling van...*

What films have you seen recently?
Welke films heeft u onlangs gezien?
wel**-ku films hayft uu on-**langs** ge-**zeen

What is (English name of film) **called in Dutch?**
Hoe heet ... in het Nederlands?
*hoo hayt ... in het **nay**-der-lands*

Who is your favourite actor / actress?
Wie is uw favoriete acteur / actrice?
*wee is uuw **fah**-vo-ree-tu **ak**-teur / **ak**-tree-cu*

■ **YOU MAY HEAR**

Uitverkocht
***uit**-ver-koCHt*
Sold out

■ **ENTERTAINMENT** ■ **LEISURE/INTERESTS**

women   **men - suits**   **shoes**

sizes	
UK	EC
10	36
12	38
14	40
16	42
18	44
20	46

sizes	
UK	EC
36	46
38	48
40	50
42	52
44	54
46	56

sizes			
UK	EC	UK	EC
2	35	8	42
3	36	9	43
4	37	10	44
5	38	11	45
6	39		
7	41		

May I try this on?
Mag ik dit proberen?
*maCH ik dit **proh**-bay-ru*

Where is the changing room?
Waar is de paskamer?
*wahr is du **pas**-kah-mer*

Have you a bigger size?
Heeft u een grotere maat?
*hayft uu un **groh**-tu-ru maht*

Have you a smaller size?
Heeft u een kleinere maat?
*hayft uu un **klei**-nu-ru maht*

Do you have this...?
Heeft u dit...?
hayft uu dit...

in my size
in mijn maat
in mein maht

in other colours
in andere kleuren
*in **an**-du-ru **kleu**-ru*

That's a shame!
Dat is jammer!
*dat is **yam**-mer*

It's too short
Het is te kort
het is tu kort

It's too long
Het is te lang
het is tu lang

I'm just looking
Ik kijk alleen
*ik keik al-**layn***

I'll take it
Ik neem het
ik naym het

■ **YOU MAY HEAR**

Welke maat
wel-ku maht
What size?

Past het?
past het
Does it fit you?

■ **NUMBERS** ■ **PAYING** ■ **SHOPPING**

COTTON	KATOEN, HET	SILK	ZIJDE, DE
LACE	KANT, DE	SUEDE	SUEDE, HET
LEATHER	LEER, HET	WOOL	WOL, DE

belt	riem, de	reem
blouse	blouse, de	bloos
bra	beha, de	**bay**-hah
coat	jas, de	yas
dress	jurk, de	yurk
gloves	handschoenen, de	**hand**-schoo-nu
hat	hoed, de	hood
hat *(woollen)*	muts, de	muts
jacket	jasje, het	**ya**-shu
nightdress	nachtjapon, de	**naCHt**-yah-pon
pyjamas	pyjama, de	**pee**-yah-mah
raincoat	regenjas, de	**ray**-CHu-yas
sandals	sandalen, de	san-**dah**-lu
scarf *(woollen)*	das, de	das
shirt	overhemd, het	**oh**-ver-hemd
shorts	korte broek, de	**kor**-tu brook
skirt	rok, de	rok
slippers	slippers, de	**slip**-pers
socks	sokken, de	**sok**-ku
suit	kostuum / pak, het	kos-**tuum** / pak
swimsuit	zwempak, het	**zwem**-pak
tie	stropdas, de	**strop**-das
tights	panties / kousen, de	pan-**tees** / **kou**-su
tracksuit	trainingspak, het	**tray**-nings-pak
trousers	broek, de	brook
t-shirt	t-shirt, het	tee-shirt
underpants	onderbroek, de	**on**-der-brook
underwear	ondergoed, het	**on**-der-CHood
vest	hemd, het	hemd
zip	ritssluiting, de	**rits**-slui-ting

27

> Two key words for describing colours in Dutch are:
> **licht** light   **donker** dark

black	zwart	zwart
blue	blauw	blouw
navy blue	marine blauw	mah-**ree**-nu blouw
brown	bruin	bruin
cream	crème	krem
crimson	vuurrood	**vuur**-rohd
gold	goud	CHoud
green	groen	CHroon
grey	grijs	CHreis
orange	oranje	**oh**-ran-yu
pink	rose	ro-su
dark pink	oudrose	**oud**-ro-su
light pink	lichtrose	**liCHt**-ro-su
purple	paars	pahrs
red	rood	rohd
silver	zilver	**zil**-ver
white	wit	wit
yellow	geel	CHayl

■ SHAPE

big	groot	CHroht
fat	dik	dik
flat	plat	plat
long	lang	lang
narrow	smal	smal
round	rond	rond
small	klein	klein
square	vierkant	**veer**-kant
tall	lang / groot	lang / CHroht
thick	dik	dik
thin	dun	dun
tiny	heel klein	hayl klein
wide	wijd	weid

This doesn't work
Het werkt niet
het werkt neet

The ... doesn't work
De/Het ... werkt niet
du/het ... werkt neet

The ... don't work
De ... werken niet
*du ... **wer**-ku niet*

light
het licht
het liCHt

heating
de verwarming
*du ver-**war**-ming*

air conditioning
de air-conditioning
*du **air**-con-di-ti-oh-ning*

There's a problem with the room
Er is een probleem met de kamer
*er is un **proh**-blaym met du **kah**-mer*

It's noisy (room)
Er is teveel lawaai
*er is tu-**vayl lah**-wahee*

It's too hot (room)
Het is te warm
het is tu warm

It's too cold
Het is te koud
het is tu koud

It's too hot / too cold (food)
Het is te heet / te koud
het is tu hayt / tu koud

The meat is cold
Het vlees is koud
het vlays is koud

This isn't what I have ordered
Dit is niet wat ik heb besteld
*dit is neet wat ik heb bu-**steld***

To whom should I complain?
Bij wie kan ik mij beklagen?
*bɔi wee kan ik mei bu-**klah**-CHu*

It's faulty
Het is defect
*het is du-**fect***

I want a refund
Ik wil mijn geld terug
*ik wil mein CHeld tu-**ruCH***

The goods were damaged during transport
De goederen zijn beschadigd tijdens het transport
*du **CHoo**-du-ru zein bu-**schah**-diCHd **tei**-dens het **trans**-port*

■ PROBLEMS ■ REPAIRS ■ ROOM SERVICE

COMPUTER	COMPUTER, DE
DATABASE	DATABASE, DE / GEGEVENSBESTAND, HET
FILE	FILE, DE / ARCHIEF, HET
FLOPPY DISK	FLOPPY DISK, DE / SCHIJF, DE
HARD DISK	HARDE SCHIJF, DE
KEYBOARD	TOETSENBORD, HET
PRINT-OUT	PRINT, DE
SCREEN	SCHERM, HET

What computer do you use?
Welke computer gebruikt u?
wel-ku com-pyuu-ter CHu-bruikt uu

Do you have an electronic mailbox?
Heeft u een elektronische postbus?
hayft uu un ay-lek-troh-nee-schu post-bus

What is your number?
Wat is uw nummer?
wat is uuw num-mer

Do you have a database?
Heeft u een database?
hayft uu un dah-tah-bays

Can you send it on a floppy disk?
Kunt u het op een floppydisk sturen?
kunt uu het op un flop-pee-disk stuu-ru

What word processing package do you use?
Welk tekstverwerkingsprogramma gebruikt u?
welk tekst-ver-wer-kings-proh-CHram-mah CHu-bruikt uu

How much memory does the computer have?
Hoe groot is het geheugen van de computer?
hoe CHroht is het CHu-heu-CHu van du com-pyuu-ter

■ OFFICE

*With the single European Market, European Union (EU) citizens are
subject only to highly selective spot checks and they can go
through the blue customs channel (unless they have goods to
declare). There is no restriction, either by quantity or value, on
goods purchased by travellers in another EU country provided they
are **for their own personal use** (guidelines have been published).
If you are unsure of certain items, check with the customs officials
as to whether payment of duty is required.*

PASPOORTCONTROLE	PASSPORT CONTROL
EU	EU
DOUANE	CUSTOMS

Do I have to pay duty on this?
  Moet ik hiervoor invoerrecthten betalen?
  *moot ik **heer**-vohr in-**voor**-rech-tu be-**tah**-lu*

This is a gift
  Dit is een cadeau
  *dit is un kah-**doh***

It is for my own personal use
  Het is voor mijn persoonlijk gebruik
  *het is vohr mein per-**sohn**-luk CHu-**bruik***

We are on our way to... *(if in transit through a country)*
  Wij zijn op weg naar...
  wei zein op weCH nahr...

The children are on this passport
  De kinderen staan op dit paspoort
  *du **kin**-du-ru stahn op dit **pas**-port*

The Netherlands is an excellent place for cycling. The country is flat and there are cycling paths along most main roads. In the cities, car drivers are used to cyclists, but you must remain careful. There are special cycle routes and organized tours into the countryside.

I want to hire a bicycle
Ik wil een fiets huren
*ik wil un feets **huu**-ru*

How much is the deposit?
Hoeveel is de waarborgsom?
*hoo-vayl is du **wahr**-borCH-som*

Has the bicycle...?	**gears**	**breaks**	**lights**
Heeft de fiets...?	versnellingen	remmen	licht
hayft du feets...	*ver-**snel**-ling-u*	***rem**-mu*	*liCHt*

When is the bicycle due back?
Wanneer moet de fiets terug?
*wan-**nayr** moot du feets tu-**RuCH***

Are there any organized tours?
Zijn er georganiseerde fietstochten?
*zein er CHu-or-CHah-nee-**sayr**-du **feets**-toCH-tu*

How long is the tour?
Hoe lang duurt de tocht?
hoo lang duurt du toCHt

Where/When does it start?
Waar/Hoe laat begint het?
*wahr/hoo laht be-**CHint** het*

My tyre is flat
Ik heb een lekke band
*ik heb un **lek**-ku band*

Can you repair it?
Kunt u hem plakken?
*kunt uu hem **plak**-ku*

Have you a...?	**pump**	**repair kit**	**new tube**
Heeft u een...?	fietspomp	reparatieset	nieuwe band
hayft uu un...	***feets**-pomp*	*ray-pah-**rah**-tsee-set*	***nee**-wu band*

■ **YOU MAY HEAR**

Kijk uit!
keik uit!
Look out!

Richting aangeven, alstublieft
*ri**CH**-ting **ahn**-gay-vu als-tuu-**bleeft***
Indicate, please

days

MONDAY	MAANDAG
TUESDAY	DINSDAG
WEDNESDAY	WOENSDAG
THURSDAY	DONDERDAG
FRIDAY	VRIJDAG
SATURDAY	ZATERDAG
SUNDAY	ZONDAG

seasons

SPRING	LENTE, DE / VOORJAAR, HET
SUMMER	ZOMER, DE
AUTUMN	HERFST, DE
WINTER	WINTER, DE

months

JANUARY	JANUARI
FEBRUARY	FEBRUARI
MARCH	MAART
APRIL	APRIL
MAY	MEI
JUNE	JUNI
JULY	JULI
AUGUST	AUGUSTUS
SEPTEMBER	SEPTEMBER
OCTOBER	OKTOBER
NOVEMBER	NOVEMBER
DECEMBER	DECEMBER

What's the date?
Wat is de datum?
*wat is du **dah**-tum*

What day is it today?
Welke dag is het vandaag?
wel**-ku daCH is het van-**dahCH

It's the 5th of August 1994
Het is 5 augustus 1994
*het is veif ou-**Chus**-tus nay-CHen-teen-**veer**-en-**nay**-CHen-tiCH*

on Saturday
op zaterdag
*op **zah**-ter-daCH*

on Saturdays
's zaterdags
*s-**zah**-ter-daCHs*

every Saturday
iedere zaterdag
***ee**-du-ru **zah**-ter-daCH*

this Saturday
deze zaterdag
***day**-zu **zah**-ter-daCH*

next / last Saturday
volgende / vorige zaterdag
***vol**-CHen-du / **vo**-ri CHu **zah**-ter-daCH*

in June
in juni
*in **juu**-nee*

at the beginning / end of June
begin / eind juni
*bu-**CHin** / eind **juu**-nee*

before summer
voor de zomer
*vohr du **zoh**-mer*

during the summer
tijdens de zomer
*tei-dens du **zoh**-mer*

after summer
na de zomer
*nah du **zoh**-mer*

■ NUMBERS

I need a dentist
Ik heb een tandarts nodig
*ik heb un **tand**-arts noh-diCH*

He / She has toothache
Hij / Zij heeft kiespijn
*hei / zei hayft **kees**-pein*

Can you do a temporary filling?
Kunt u een tijdelijke vulling maken?
*kunt uu un **tei**-du-lu-ku **vul**-ling **mah**-ku*

It hurts (me)
Het doet pijn
het doot pein

Can you give me something for the pain?
Kunt u mij iets tegen de pijn geven?
*kunt uu mei eets **tay**-CHu du pein **CHay**-vu*

I think I have an abscess
Ik geloof dat ik een gezwel heb
*ik CHu-**lohf** dat ik un CHu-**zwel** heb*

Can you repair my dentures?
Kunt u mijn kunstgebit repareren?
*kunt uu mein **kunst**-CHu-bit ray-pah-**ray**-ru*

Do I have to pay?
Moet ik betalen?
*moot ik bu-**tah**-lu*

How much will it be?
Hoeveel kost het?
***hoo**-vayl kost het*

I need a receipt for my insurance
Ik heb een ontvangstbewijs nodig voor mijn verzekering
*ik heb un ont-**vangst**-bu-weis **noh**-diCH vohr mein ver-**zay**-ke-ring*

■ YOU MAY HEAR

Hij moet er uit
hei moot er uit
It has to come out

Ik ga u een injectie geven
*ik CHah uu un in-**yec**-tsee*
I'm going to give you an injection

OPPOSITE	TEGENOVER	*tay*-CHu-oh-ver
NEXT TO	NAAST	na*h*ıst
NEAR TO	VLAKBIJ	*vlak*-bei
TRAFFIC LIGHTS	STOPLICHTEN, DE	*stop*-liCH-tu
AT THE CORNER	OP DE HOEK	op du hook

Excuse me, sir / madam!
Pardon meneer / mevrouw!
par-don mu-*nayr* / mu-*vrouw*

How do I get...?
Hoe kom ik...?
hoo kom ik...

to the station
bij het station
bei het stah-shon

to the Rijksmuseum
bij het Rijksmuseum
bei het reiks-muu-say-yum

to the Dam square
op de Dam
op du dam

We're looking for...
Wij zoeken...
wei zoo-ku...

Is it far?
Is het ver?
is het ver

Can I walk there?
Kan ik er heen lopen?
kan ik er hayn loh-pu

We're lost
Wij zijn verdwaald
wei zein ver-dwahld

Is this the right way to...?
Is dit de goede weg naar...?
is dit du CHoo-du weCH nahr...

How do I get onto the motorway?
Hoe kom ik op de autoweg?
hoo kom ik op du ou-toh-weCH

Can you show me where it is on the map?
Kunt u mij laten zien waar het op de kaart is?
kunt uu mei lah-tu zeen wahr het op du kahrt is

■ YOU MAY HEAR

Na de brug
nah du bruCH
After the bridge

Ga links / rechts
CHah links / reCHts
Turn left / right

Ga rechtdoor totdat u bij ... komt
CHah reCHt-dor tot-dat uu bei ... komt
Keep straight on until you get to...

■ BASICS ■ MAPS, GUIDES & NEWSPAPERS

What facilities do you have for disabled people?
Welke faciliteiten heeft u voor invaliden?
*wel-ku fah-cee-lee-**tei**-tu hayft uu vohr in-vah-**lee**-du*

Are there any toilets for the disabled?
Zijn er toiletten voor invaliden?
*zein er twa-**let**-tu vohr in-vah-**lee**-du*

Do you have any bedrooms on the ground floor?
Heeft u slaapkamers op de begane grond?
*hayft uu **slahp**-kah-mers op du bu-**CHa**-nu CHrond*

Is there a lift?
Is er een lift?
is er un lift

Where is the lift?
Waar is de lift?
wahr is du lift

Are there any ramps?
Zijn er hellende opritten?
*zein er **hel**-len-du **op**-rit-tu*

How many stairs are there?
Hoeveel trappen zijn er?
*hoo-vayl **trap**-pu zein er*

How wide is the entrance door?
Hoe breed is de ingang?
*hoe brayd is du **in**-CHang*

Where is the wheelchair-accessible entrance?
Waar is de ingang voor rolstoelen?
*wahr is du **in**-CHang vohr **rol**-stoo-lu*

Is there a reduction for handicapped people?
Is er korting voor gehandicapten?
*is er **kor**-ting vohr CHu-**hen**-dee-cap-tu*

Is there somewhere I can sit down?
Kan ik ergens zitten?
*kan ik **er**-CHens **zit**-tu*

■ **ACCOMMODATION** ■ **HOTEL**

ZIEKENHUIS	HOSPITAL
ONGEVALLEN	CASUALTY DEPARTMENT
SPREEKUUR	SURGERY HOURS

I need a doctor
Ik moet naar de dokter
*ik moot nahr du **dok**-tur*

I have pain here *(point)*
Het doet hier pijn
het doot heer pein

My son / daughter is ill
Mijn zoon / dochter is ziek
*mein zohn / **doCH**-tur is zeek*

He / She has a temperature
Hij / Zij heeft koorts
hei / zei hayft kohrts

I'm diabetic
Ik heb suikerziekte
*ik heb **sui**-kur-zeek-tu*

I'm pregnant
Ik ben in verwachting
*ik ben in ver-**waCH**-ting*

I'm allergic to penicillin
Ik ben allergisch voor penicilline
*ik ben al-**ler**-CHeesch voor pay-nu-cil-**lee**-nu*

I'm on the pill
Ik gebruik de pil
ik CHu-bruik du pil

My blood group is...
Mijn bloedgroep is...
*mein **blood**-CHroop is...*

Will he / she have to go to hospital?
Moet hij / zij naar het ziekenhuis?
*moot hei / zei nahr het **zee**-ku-huis*

Will I have to pay?
Moet ik betalen?
*\moot ik bu-**tah**-lu*

How much will it cost?
Hoeveel kost het?
*h**oo**-vayl kost het*

I need a receipt for the insurance
Ik heb een ontvangstbewijs nodig voor de verzekering
*ik heb un ont-**vangst**-bu-weis **noh**-diCH vohr du ver-**zay**-ku-ring*

■ **YOU MAY HEAR**

Het is niet ernstig
*het is neet **ern**-stiCH*
It's not serious

■ **BODY** ■ **EMERGENCIES** ■ **PHARMACY**

> If you want black coffee ask for **zwarte koffie**. For a white coffee
> ask for **koffie met melk**.
> Dutch lager is called **bier** or **pils** and is usually served with a small
> head of foam.

a coffee	a lager	a glass of white wine	...please
een koffie	een pils	een glaas witte vijn	...alstublieft
un *kof-fee*	un pils	un CHlas *vit*-tu vein	...als-tuu-**bleeft**

a tea...	with milk	with lemon	no sugar
een thee...	met melk	met citroen	geen suiker
un tay...	met melk	met cee-**troon**	CHayn *sui*-kur

for me	for him / her	for us
voor mij	voor hem / haar	voor ons
vohr mei	vohr hem / hahr	vohr ons

with ice, please
met ijs, alstublieft
met eis als-tuu-**bleeft**

A bottle of mineral water	sparkling	still
Een fles mineraalwater	met koolzuur	zonder koolzuur
un fles mee-nu-**rahl**-wah-ter	met **kohl**-zuur	**zon**-der **kohl**-zuur

Would you like a drink?
Wilt u iets drinken?
wilt uu eets **drin**-ku

I'm very thirsty	It's my round!
Ik heb erge dorst	Dit is mijn rondje
ik heb **er**-CHu dorst	dit is mein **ron**-chu

■ **OTHER DRINKS TO TRY**

advocaat *Dutch liqueur based on egg yolks*

chocolademelk *hot or cold chocolate drink*

jenever *Dutch gin:* **jonge** *young,* **oude** *old (smooth)*

rode wijn *red wine*

witte wijn *white wine*

■ **EATING OUT**

For those who are vegetarian, or who prefer vegetarian dishes, turn to the VEGETARIAN topic for further phrases.

Where can I have a snack?
Waar kan ik wat eten?
*wahr kan ik wat **ay**-tu*

not too expensive
niet te duur
neet tu duur

Can you recommend a good restaurant?
Kunt u een goed restaurant aanbevelen?
*kunt uu un CHood res-tou-**rant** ahn-bu-**vay**-lu*

I'd like a table for ... people
Ik wil graag een tafel voor ... personen
*ik wil CHrahCH un **tah**-fel vohr ... per-**soh**-nu*

for tonight
voor vanavond
*vohr van-**ah**-vond*

for tomorrow night
voor morgenavond
*vohr **mor**-CHen-ah-vond*

at 9 pm
om 9 uur
*om **nay**-CHu uur*

The menu, please
Het menu, alstublieft
*het mu-**nuu** als-tuu-**bleeft***

What is the dish of the day?
Wat is de dagschotel?
*wat is du **daCH**-schoh-tel*

Do you have...?
Heeft u...?
hayft u...

à la carte menu
een à la carte menu
*un ah lah kart mu-**nuu***

a children's menu
een kindermenu
*un **kin**-der-mu-nuu*

What can you recommend?
Wat kunt u aanbevelen?
*wat kunt uu ahn-bu-**vay**-lu*

What is this?
Wat is dit?
wat is dit

I'll have this
Ik wil dit
ik wil dit

Excuse me!
Pardon!
*par-**don**!*

Please bring...
Alstublieft, breng...
*als-tuu-**bleeft** breng...*

more bread
meer brood
mayr brohd

more water
meer water
*mayr **wah**-ter*

another bottle
nog een fles
noCH un fles

the bill
de rekening
*du **ray**-ku-ning*

Is service included?
Is de bediening inbegrepen?
*is du bu-**dee**-ning in-bu-CHray-pu*

CONT.

■ EATING PLACES

Most bars or pubs serve snacks, filled rolls and light meals.
A bar or pub is usually called café.
Snackbars serve fast food.
Cafeterias serve light meals.
There are a few traditional Dutch restaurants but many specialize
in foreign food such as Chinese and Indonesian.

■ VOORGERECHTEN STARTERS/APPETIZERS

What starters do you have?
Welke voorgerechten heeft u?
wel-ku vohr-CHu-reCH-tu hayft uu

■ VLEES

VLEES	MEAT
biefstuk	fillet steak
eend	duck
entrecote	entrecôte steak
escalope	veal escalope
haas	hare
kip	chicken
konijn	rabbit
koteletten	chops
lamsvlees	lamb
niertjes	kidney
patrijs	partridge
rosbief	roast beef
varkensvlees	pork

■ VIS

VIS	FISH
aal	eel
forel	trout
garnalen	prawns
haring	herring (raw / marinated)
kabeljauw	cod
kreeft	lobster
mosselen	mussels

paling	eel (often smoked)
sardientjes	sardines
schelvis	haddock
schol	plaice
tong	sole
tonijn	tuna
zalm	salmon
zwaardvis	swordfish

■ GROENTE — VEGETABLES

asperges	asparagus
aubergines	aubergines
komkommer	cucumber
paprikas	peppers
patat frites	chips
salade	usually lettuce, tomatoes and cucumber
sla	lettuce
snijbonen	french beans
spinazie	spinach
tuinbonen	broad beans
tomaten	tomatoes
uien	onions

■ NAGERECHT — DESSERTS

What desserts do you have?
Welke nagerechten heeft u?
wel-ku nah-CHu-reCh-tu hayft uu

fruit	fruit
gebak	cake
ijs	ice cream
kaas	cheese

What cheeses do you have?
Wat voor kaas heeft u?
wat vohr kahs hayft uu

belegen/jonge kaas	matured/young cheese
oude kaas	old cheese

POLITIE	POLICE
AMBULANCE	AMBULANCE
BRANDWEER	FIRE BRIGADE
ONGEVALLEN	CASUALTY DEPARTMENT
EHBO	FIRST AID (sign)

Help!
Help!
help!

Fire!
Brand!
brand!

Can you help me?
Kunt u mij helpen?
*kunt uu mei **hel**-pu*

There's been an accident!
Er is een ongeluk gebeurd!
*er is un **on**-CHu-luk CHu-**beurd**!*

Someone is injured
Er is iemand gewond
*er is **ee**-mand CHu-**wond***

Someone has been knocked down by a car
Er is iemand overreden
*er is **ee**-mand **oh**-ver-ray-du*

Phone...
Bel...
bel...

the police
de politie
*du poh-**lee**-tsee*

an ambulance
een ambulance
*un am-**buu**-lan-cu*

please
alstublieft
*als-tuu-**bleeft***

Where is the police station?
Waar is het politiebureau?
*wahr is het poh-**lee**-tsee-buu-roh*

I want to report a theft
Ik wil een diefstal aangeven
*ik wil un **deef**-stal ahn-CHay-vu*

I've been robbed / attacked
Ik ben beroofd / aangevallen
*ik ben be-**rohfd** / **aan**-CHu-val-lu*

They've stolen my...
Ze hebben mijn ... gestolen
*zu **heb**-bu mein ... CHu-**stoh**-lu*

bag
tas
tas

traveller's cheques
travellercheques
trah-vel-ler-cheks

My car has been broken into
Mijn auto is ingebroken
*mein **ou**-toh is in-CHu-**broh**-ku*

My car radio has been stolen
  Mijn autoradio is gestolen
  *mein **ou**-toh-rah-di-oh is CHu-**stoh**-lu*

I've been raped
  Ik ben verkracht
  *ik ben ver-**kraCHt***

I want to speak to a policewoman
  Ik wil met een politie-agente spreken
  *ik wil met un poh-**lee**-tsee-ah-CHen-tu **spray**-ku*

I need to make an urgent telephone call
  Ik moet dringend opbellen
  *ik moot dring-**end op**-bel-lu*

I need a report for my insurance
  Ik heb een rapport nodig voor mijn verzekering
  *ik heb un rap-**port** noh-diCH vohr mein ver-**zay**-ku-ring*

I don't know the speed limit
  Ik weet de maximum snelheid niet
  *ik wayt du max-**ee**-mum **snel**-heid neet*

How much is the fine?
  Hoeveel bedraagt de boete?
  ***hoo**-vayl bu-**drahCHt** du **boo**-tu*

Where do I pay it?
  Waar moet ik betalen?
  *wahr moot ik bu-**tah**-lu*

Do I have to pay it straightaway?
  Moet ik het direct betalen?
  *moot ik het dee-**rekt** be-**tah**-lu*

I'm very sorry
  Het spijt me heel erg
  het speit mu hayl erCH

■ **YOU MAY HEAR**

U reed door het rode licht
*uu rayd dohr het **roh**-du liCHt*
You went through a red light

■ **BODY** ■ **DOCTOR**

43

*Tourist Information Offices (**VVV**), local and national newspapers can provide information about events and entertainment.*

What is there to do in the evenings?
Wat is er s'avonds te doen?
*wat is er **sah**-vonds tu doon*

Do you know what events are on this week?
Weet u welke evenementen er deze week zijn?
*wayt uu **wel**-ku ay-vu-nu-**men**-tu er **day**-zu wayk zijn*

Is there anything for children?
Is er iets voor kinderen?
*is er eets vohr **kin**-du-ru*

Where can I get tickets...?
Waar kan ik kaartjes krijgen...?
*wahr kan ik **kahr**-chus **krei**-CHu...*

for tonight
voor vanavond
*vohr van-**ah**-vond*

for the show
voor de voorstelling
*vohr du **vohr**-stel-ling*

for the football match
voor de voetbalwedstrijd
*vohr du **voot**-bal-wed-streid*

I'd like ... tickets
Ik wil graag ... kaartjes
*ik wil CHrahCH ... **kahr**-chus*

...adults
...volwassenen
*...vol-**was**-su-nu*

...children
...kinderen
*...**kin**-du-ru*

Where can we go dancing?
Waar kunnen we dansen?
*wahr **kun**-nu wu **dan**-su*

What time does it open?
Hoe laat gaat het open?
*hoo laht CHaht het **oh**-pu*

How much is it to get in?
Hoeveel is de entree?
hoo**-vayl is du an-**tray

■ **YOU MAY HEAR**

De toegang is ... gulden
*de **too**-CHang is ... **CHul**-du*
Entry is ... guilders

■ CINEMA ■ SIGHTSEEING & TOURIST OFFICE ■ THEATRE

*To fax the Netherlands from the UK, the code is **00 31** followed by the Dutch area code, e.g. Amsterdam **20**, Rotterdam **10**, The Hague **70** and then the fax number you require.*

ADDRESSING A FAX	
FROM	VAN
FOR THE ATTENTION OF	TEN AANZIEN VAN
DATE	DATUM
THIS DOCUMENT CONTAINS ...	DIT DOCUMENT HEEFT ...
PAGES INCLUDING THIS	BLADZIJDEN INCLUSIEF DIT BLAD

Do you have a fax?
Heeft u een fax?
hayft u un fax

I want to send a fax
Ik wil een fax sturen
*ik wil un fax **stuu**-ru*

What is your fax number?
Wat is uw faxnummer?
*wat is uuw **fax**-num-mer*

I am having trouble getting through to your fax
Ik heb moeilijkheden om uw fax te bereiken
*ik heb **mooee**-lik-hay-du om uuw fax tu bu-**rei**-ku*

Resend your fax, please
Stuur uw fax nog een keer, alstublieft
*stuur uuw fax noCH un kayr als-tuu-**bleeft***

I can't read it
Ik kan het niet lezen
*ik kan het neet **lay**-zu*

The fax is constantly engaged
De fax is steeds bezet
*du fax is stayds bu-**zet***

Can I send a fax from here?
Kan ik hier een fax versturen?
*kan ik heer un fax ver-**stuu**-ru*

■ LETTERS ■ TELEPHONE

*In the spring the Dutch bulb fields between Haarlem and The Hague (the coastal area in the western part of the Netherlands) are in full bloom. A well-known centre is the **Keukenhof**. Traditionally the main growers of fresh flowers can be found around Aalsmeer, just south of Amsterdam.*

I want information on the bulb fields
Ik wil informatie over de bloembollenvelden
*ik wil in-for-**mah**-tsee oh-ver de **bloom**-bol-lu-vel-du*

Are there organized daytrips / tours?
Zijn er georganiseerde dagtochten / rondleidingen?
*zein er gu-or-gah-nee-**sayr**-du **daCH**-toCH-tu / **rond**-lei-ding-u*

When / Where is the flower festival?
Wanneer / Waar is het bloemencorso?
*wan-**nayr** / wahr is het **bloo**-mu-cor-soh*

Does the procession come here?
Komt de stoet hier voorbij?
*komt du stoot heer vohr-**bei***

Where is the best place to watch?
Waar is de beste plaats om te kijken?
*wahr is de **bes**-tu plahts om tu **kei**-ku*

Your flowers are beautiful
Uw bloemen zijn mooi
*uuw **bloo**-mu zein mohee*

I want bulbs for...	tulips	daffodils
Ik wil bloembollen voor...	tulpen	narcissen
*ik wil **bloom**-bol-lu vohr...*	*tul-pu*	*nar-**cis**-su*

Do you have...?	fresias	roses	carnations
Heeft u...?	fresia's	rozen	anjers
hayft u...	***fray**-see-ahs*	***roh**-zu*	***an**-yurs*

■ YOU MAY HEAR

Een bos bloemen	Een boeket	Tuinder
*un bos **bloo**-mu*	*un bos-**ket***	***tuin**-der*
A bunch of flowers	A bouquet	Grower *(farmer)*

biscuits	koekjes, de	**kook**-yes
bread	brood, het	brohd
bread (brown)	bruinbrood, het	**bruin**-brohd
bread roll	broodje, het	**brohd**-yu
butter	boter, de	**boh**-ter
cereal	cornflakes, de	**corn**-flayks
cheese	kaas, de	kahs
chicken	kip, de	kip
chips	patat frites	**pah**-tat freet
coffee	koffie, de	**kof**-fee
cream	(slag)room, de	(slaCH)rohm
crisps	chips, de	chips
eggs	eieren, de	**ei**-yu-ru
flour	bloem, de	bloom
ham (cooked)	gekookte ham, de	CHu-**kohk**-tu ham
ham (cured)	gerookte ham, de	CHu-**rohk**-tu ham
herbal tea	kruidenthee, de	**krui**-du-tay
honey	honing, de	**hoh**-ning
jam	jam, de	shem
margarine	margarine, de	mar-**CHah**-ree-ne
marmalade	marmelade, de	mar-mu-**lah**-du
milk	melk, de	melk
mustard	mosterd, de	**mos**-turd
olive oil	olijfolie, de	**oh**-leif-oh-lee
orange juice	sinaasappelsap, het	**see**-nas-ap-pel-sap
pepper	peper, de	**pay**-per
rice	rijst, de	reist
salt	zout, het	zout
stock cube	bouillonblokje, het	**bool**-yon-blok-yu
sugar	suiker, de	**sui**-kur
tea	thee, de	tay
tinned tomatoes	tomaten in blik, de	**toh**-mah-tu in blik
vinegar	azijn, de	**ah**-zein
yoghurt	yoghurt, de	**yoCH**-hurt

■ FRUIT

apples	appels, de	*ap*-pels
apricots	abrikozen, de	ah-bree-**koh**-zu
bananas	bananen, de	bah-**nah**-nu
cherries	kersen, de	*ker*-su
grapefruit	grapefruit, de	**CH**rayp-fruit
grapes	druiven, de	*drui*-vu
lemon	citroen, de	cee-**troon**
melon	meloen, de	mu-**loon**
nectarines	nectarines, de	nek-**tah**-ree-nus
oranges	sinaasappels, de	**see**-nas-ap-pels
peaches	perziken, de	**per**-zi-ku
pears	peren, de	**pay**-ru
pineapple	ananas, de	a-**nah**-nas
plums	pruimen, de	**prui**-mu
raspberries	frambozen, de	fram-**boh**-zu
strawberries	aardbeien, de	**ahrd**-bei-yu

■ VEGETABLES

asparagus	asperges, de	as-**per**-shus
carrots	worteltjes/peentjes, de	**wor**-tel-chus / **payn**-chus
cauliflower	bloemkool, de	**bloom**-kohl
courgettes	courgettes, de	**koor**-shet-tus
cucumber	komkommer, de	**kom**-kom-mer
french beans	snijbonen, de	**snei**-boh-nu
garlic	knoflook, de	**knof**-lohk
leek	prei, de	prei
lettuce	sla, de	slah
mushrooms	champignons, de	sham-ping-**yons**
onions	uien, de	**ui**-yu
peas	doperwten, de	**dop**-er-tu
peppers	paprika's, de	**pah**-pree-kahs
potatoes	aardappels, de	**ahrd**-ap-pels
spinach	spinazie, de	spee-**nah**-zee
tomatoes	tomaten, de	toh-**mah**-tu

Where / When is the football match?
Waar / wanneer is de voetbalwedstrijd?
*wahr / wan-**nayr** is du **voot**-bal-wed-streid*

Is it on TV?
Is het op tv?
is het op tay-vay

Where can we buy tickets?
Waar kunnen we kaartjes kopen?
*wahr **kun**-nu wu **kahr**-chus **koh**-pu*

Will tickets be for sale in advance?
Is er voorverkoop?
*is er vohr-**ver**-kohp*

How do we get to the stadium?
Hoe komen we bij het stadion?
*hoo **koh**-mu wu bei het **stah**-dee-yon*

What time is kick-off?
Hoe laat is de aftrap?
*hoo laht is du **af**-trap*

Which is your favourite team? *(familiar)*
Wat is jouw favoriete team?
*wat is youw fah-vo-**ree**-tu teem*

My team is...
Mijn team is...
mein teem is...

My favourite player is...
Mijn favoriete speler is...
*mein fah-vo-**ree**-tu **spay**-ler is ..*

■ **YOU MAY HEAR**

Goed gedaan!
*CHood CHu-**dahn**!*
Well done!

Wat jammer!
*wat **yam**-mer!*
What a shame!

Hup...
hup...
Come on...

■ **LEISURE/INTERESTS** ■ **SPORT**

*You will often find the Dutch quite formal in their greetings, shaking hands both on meeting and parting. Frequent greetings include **goedendag**, **meneer** or **goedendag**, **mevrouw**. If you are saying good night and leaving you would say **goedenavond**, **welterusten**.*

Hello!
Hallo!
*hal-**loh**!*

Goodbye!
Dag!
daCH!

Good morning (until 12.00)
Goedemorgen
***CH**oo-du-mor-CHu*

Good afternoon
Goedemiddag
***CH**oo-du-mid-daCH*

Good evening (from 1800 until 2400)
Goedenavond
***CH**oo-du-ah-vond*

Good evening / Good night (after 2400)
Goedenacht
***CH**oo-du-naCHt*

Pleased to meet you
Aangenaam kennis te maken
*ahn-CHu-nahm **ken**-nis tu **mah**-ku*

It's a pleasure
Prettig u te ontmoeten
***pret**-tiCH uu tu ont-**moo**-tu*

How are you?
Hoe gaat het met u?
hoo CHaht het met uu

Fine, thanks
Goed, dank u
CHood dank uu

And you?
En met u?
en met uu

How are things?
Hoe gaat het?
hoo CHaat het

See you tomorrow
Tot morgen
*tot **mor**-CHu*

See you later
Tot straks
tot straks

Until we meet again
Tot ziens
tot zeens

■ **BASICS** ■ **MAKING FRIENDS**

These phrases are intended for use at the hotel desk. More details about rooms can be found in the ACCOMMODATION topic.

Do you have a room for tonight?
Heeft u een kamer voor vannacht?
*hayft uu un **kah**-mer vohr van-**naCHt***

I booked a room...
Ik heb een kamer gereserveerd...
*ik heb un **kah**-mer CHu-**ray**-ser-vayrd...*

in the name of...
op naam van...
op nahm van...

I'd like to see the room
Ik wil de kamer graag zien
*ik wil du **kah**-mer CHrahCH zeen*

Have you anything else?
Heeft u iets anders?
*hayft uu eets **an**-ders*

Where can I park the car?
Waar kan ik de auto parkeren?
*wahr kan ik du **ou**-toh par-**kay**-ru*

What time is...?
Hoe laat is het...?
hoo laht is het...

dinner
diner
*dee-**nay***

breakfast
ontbijt
*ont-**beit***

We'll be back late tonight
Wij komen vanavond laat terug
*wei **koh**-mu van-**ah**-vond laht tu-**ruCH***

Do you lock the door?
Doet u de deur op slot?
doot uu du deur op slot

The key for room number...
De sleutel voor kamer nummer...
*du **sleu**-tel vohr **kah**-mer **num**-mer...*

Are there any messages for me?
Zijn er boodschappen voor mij?
*zein er **bohd**-schap-pu vohr mei*

I'm leaving tomorrow
Ik vertrek morgen
*ik ver-**trek mor**-CHu*

Prepare the bill, please
Wilt u de rekening alvast opmaken
*wilt uu du **ray**-ku-ning al-**vast** op-**mah**-ku*

Can I leave my luggage until...?
Kan ik mijn bagage hier laten tot...?
*kan ik mein bah-**CHa**-shu heer **lah**-tu tot...*

■ **ACCOMMODATION** ■ **ROOM SERVICE**

apron	schort, de	*schort*
bin	vuilnisbak, de	**vuil**-nis-bak
bin liners	vuilniszak, de	**vuil**-nis-zak
bleach	bleekwater, het	**blayk**-wah-ter
bottle opener	flessenopener, de	**fles**-su-oh-pu-ner
broom	bezem, de	**bay**-zem
can opener	blikopener, de	**blik**-oh-pu-ner
charcoal (barbecue)	houtskool, de	**houts**-kohl
dishcloth	vaatdoek, de	**vaht**-dook
dustcloth	stofdoek, de	**stof**-dook
iron	strijkijzer, de	**streik**-ei-zer
ironing board	strijkplank, de	**streik**-plank
kitchen roll	keukenrol, de	**keu**-ku-rol
matches	lucifers, de	**luu**-cee-fers
napkins (paper)	papieren zakdoekjes, de	pah-**pee**-ru zak-**dook**-yus
paper plates	papieren borden, de	pah-**pee**-ru **bor**-du
plastic cups	plastic bekertjes, de	plas-tic **bay**-ker-chus
plastic cutlery	plastic bestek, het	plas-tic bu-**stek**
rubber gloves	rubberhandschoenen, de	**rub**-ber-hand-schoo-nu
scouring pad	schuurkussentje, het	**schuur**-kus-sen-chu
soap	zeep, de	*zayp*
soap liquid (clothes)	vloeibare zeep, de	**vlooee**-bah-ru-zayp
-- powder (clothes)	zeeppoeder, het	**zayp**-poo-der
tea towel	theedoek, de	**tay**-dook
tinfoil	aluminiumfolie, de	a-luu-**mee**-nee-um foh-lee
toilet paper	toiletpapier, het	twa-**let**-pah-peer
washing-up brush	afwas borstel, de	**af**-was-bors-tel
washing-up liquid	afwasmiddel, het	**af**-was-mid-del

■ ACCOMMODATION ■ ROOM SERVICE

*The single European Market allows goods within the European Union (EU) to travel freely. Businesses which supply goods to VAT-registered EU companies are required to complete a Sales List which accompanies the goods. The VAT (BTW) registration code for the Netherlands is **NL** followed by the Dutch company's 9-digit number. VAT is paid at the rate of the destination country.*

What is your VAT registered number?
Wat is uw BTW registratienummer?

*wat is uuw bay-tay-way **ray**-CHis-trah-tee-num-mer*

Our VAT number is... *(GB followed by number)*
Ons BTW nummer is...

*ons bay-tay-way **num**-mer is...*

The goods should be delivered to *(name firm)*
De goederen moeten bezorgd worden bij...

*du **CHoo**-du-ru **moo**-tu bu-**zorCHd wor**-du bei...*

The consignment must be accompanied by an invoice
De zending moet vergezeld zijn van een faktuur

*du **zen**-ding moot ver-**CHu**-zeld zein van un fak-**tuur***

How long will it take to deliver?
Hoe lang duurt de bezorging?

*hoo lang duurt de bu-**zor**-CHing?*

Delivery will take ... days / weeks
De bezorging duurt.... dagen / weken

*du bu-**zor**-CHing duurt ... **dah**-CHu / **way**-ku*

Fax me a copy of the invoice, please
Fax mij een kopie van de faktuur, alstublieft

*fax mei un koh-**pee** van du fak-**tuur** als-tuu-**bleeft***

Confirm safe delivery of the goods, please
Bevestig de goede ontvangst van de goederen, alstublieft

*bu-**ves**-tiCH du **CHoo**-du ont-**vangst** van du **CHoo**-du ru als-tuu-**bleeft***

■ **NUMBERS** ■ **OFFICE**

STOMERIJ	DRY-CLEANER'S
WASSERETTE	LAUNDERETTE
ZEEPPOEDER	WASHING POWDER

Where can I do some washing?
Waar kan ik de was doen?
wahr kan ik du was doon

Can you send my clothes to the laundry?
Kunt u mijn kleren naar de wasserij sturen?
*kunt uu mein **klay**-ru nahr du was-su-**rei stuu**-ru*

When will my things be ready?
Wanneer zijn mijn spullen klaar?
*wan-**nayr** zein mein **spul**-lu klahr*

Is there a launderette near here?
Is er een wasserette in de buurt?
*is er un **was**-su-ret-tu in du buurt*

When does it open?
Hoe laat gaat zij open?
*hoo laht CHaht zei **oh**-pu*

When does it close?
Hoe laat gaat zij dicht?
hoo laht CHaht zei diCHt

What coins do I need?
Welke munten heb ik nodig?
*welke **mun**-tu heb ik **noh**-diCH*

Is there somewhere to dry clothes?
Is er een plek om kleren te drogen?
*is er un plek om **klay**-ru-tu **droh**-CHu*

Can you iron these clothes?
Kunt u deze kleren strijken?
*kunt uu **day**-zu **klay**-ru **strei**-ku*

Can I borrow an iron?
Kan ik een strijkijzer lenen?
*kan ik un **streik**-ei-zer **lay**-nu*

■ ROOM SERVICE

Where can I go...?
Waar kan ik...?
wahr kan ik...

fishing
vissen
vis-su

(horse) riding
paardrijden
pahrd-rei-du

skating
schaatsen
schaht-su

rollerskating
rolschaatsen
rol-schaht-su

Is there a beach near here?
Is er een strand in de buurt?
is er un strand in du buurt

Is there a swimming pool?
Is er een zwembad?
*is er un **zwem**-bad*

Where can I hire skates?
Waar kan ik schaatsen huren?
*wahr kan ik **schaht**-su **huu**-ru*

How much is it...?
Hoeveel kost het...?
hoo-vayl kost het...

per hour
per uur
per uur

per day
per dag
per daCH

What do you do in your spare time? *(familiar)*
Wat doe je in je vrije tijd?
*wat doo yu in yu **vrei**-yu teid*

I like...
Ik hou van...
ik hou van...

gardening
tuinieren
***tui**-nee-ru*

sunbathing
zonnebaden
***zon**-nu-bah-du*

We like...
Wij houden van...
*wei **hou**-du van ..*

sport
sport
sport

Do you like...? *(polite)*
Houdt u van...?
hout u van...

Do you like...? *(familiar)*
Hou jij van...?
hou yei van...

■ CINEMA ■ CYCLING ■ FLOWERS ■ FOOTBALL ■ SPORTS
■ TELEVISION ■ WALKING ■ CINEMA

17 May 1995	17 mei 1995
Dear Sirs	Geachte heren *(commercial letter)*
Dear Sir / Madam	Geachte heer / mevrouw
Yours faithfully	Hoogachtend
Dear Mr... / Mrs...	Geachte meneer... / mevrouw...
Yours sincerely	Hoogachtend
Dear Annie	Beste Annie
Best regards	Met vriendelijke groeten
Dear Jan	Lieve Jan
Love	Veel liefs

Further to your letter of 7 May...
In antwoord op uw brief van 7 mei...

Further to our telephone conversation...
Naar aanleiding van ons telefoongesprek...

Please find enclosed... *(writing on behalf of a company)*
Bijgesloten treft u aan...

Thank you for the information / your price list
Hartelijk dank voor de informatie / uw prijslijst

We are very sorry, but we are unable to...
Het spijt ons zeer, maar wij zijn niet in staat om...

I look forward to hearing from you soon
Ik hoop spoedig iets van u te mogen vernemen

by return [of] post
per omgaande

■ **FAX** ■ **OFFICE**

BAGGAGE RECLAIM	BAGAGE, DE
LEFT-LUGGAGE OFFICE	BAGAGE DEPOT, HET
LUGGAGE TROLLEY	BAGAGEWAGENTJE, HET

My luggage hasn't arrived
Mijn bagage is niet aangekomen
mein bah-CHah-shu is neet ahn-CHu-koh-mu

My suitcase has arrived damaged
Mijn koffer is beschadigd aangekomen
mein kof-fer is bu-schah-diCHd ahn-CHu-koh-mu

What's happened to the luggage on the flight from...?
Wat er gebeurd met de bagage van de vlucht uit...?
wat is er CHu-beurd met du bah-CHah-shu van du vluCHt uit...

Can you help me with my luggage, please?
Kunt u mij helpen met mijn bagage, alstublieft?
kunt uu mei hel-pu met mein bah-CHah-shu als-tuu-bleeft

When does the left-luggage office open / close?
Hoe laat gaat het bagage depot open / dicht?
hoo laht CHaht het bah-CHah-shu day-poh oh-pu / diCHt

I'd like to leave this suitcase...
Ik wil graag deze koffer hier laten...
ik wil CHrahCH day-zu kof-fer heer lah-tu...

until ... o'clock
tot ... uur
tot ... uur

overnight
tot morgen
tot mor-CHu

till Saturday
tot zaterdag
tot zah-ter-daCH

Can I leave my luggage here?
Kan ik mijn bagage hier laten?
kan ik mein bah-CHah-shu heer lah-tu

I'll collect it at... *(time)*
Ik haal het op om...
ik hahl het op om...

■ **YOU MAY HEAR**

U kunt het hier laten tot 6 uur
uu kunt het heer lah-tu tot zes uur
You may leave it here until 6 o'clock

■ **AIR TRAVEL**

57

*In this section we have used the familiar form **je** for the questions.*

What's your name?
Wat is jouw naam?
wat is jouw nahm

My name is...
Mijn naam is...
mein nahm is...

How old are you?
Hoe oud ben je?
hoo oud ben yu

I'm ... years old
Ik ben...
ik ben...

Are you Dutch? *(male/female)*
Ben je Nederlander / Nederlandse?
*ben yu **nay**-der-lan-der / **nay**-der-land-su*

I'm English / Scottish / Welsh *(male/female)*
Ik ben Engelsman / Engelse / Schot / Schotse / Wels / Welse
*ik ben **eng**-els-man / **eng**-el-su / schot / **schot**-su / wels / **wel**-su*

Where do you live?
Waar woon je?
wahr wohn yu

Where do you live? *(plural)*
Waar wonen jullie?
*wahr **woh**-nu **yul**-lee*

I live in London
Ik woon in Londen
*ik wohn in **lon**-dun*

We live in Glasgow
Wij wonen in Glasgow
*wei **woh**-nu in **glas**-gou*

I'm still studying
Ik studeer nog
*ik **stuu**-dayr noCH*

I work
Ik werk
ik werk

I'm retired
Ik ben gepensioneerd
*ik ben CHu-pen-see-oh-**nayrd***

	single	**married**	**divorced**
I'm...	alleen	getrouwd	gescheiden
Ik ben...	al-**layn**	CHu-**trouwd**	CHu-**schei**-du
ik ben...			

	a boyfriend	**a girlfriend**	**a partner**
I have...	een vriend	een vriendin	een partner
Ik heb...	un vreend	un vreen-**din**	un **part**-ner
ik heb...			

I have ... children
Ik heb ... kinderen
*ik heb ... **kin**-du-ru*

I have no children
Ik heb geen kinderen
*ik heb CHayn **kin**-du-ru*

	on holiday	**for work**
I'm here...	op vakantie	om te werken
Ik ben hier...	op vah-**kan**-tsee	om tu **wer**-ku
ik ben heer...		

Do you have a map of (town) **?**
Heeft u een plattegrond van...?
hayft u un plat-tu-CHrond van...

Can you show me where ... is on the map?
Kunt u mij laten zien waar ... is op de kaart?
kunt uu mei lah-tu zeen wahr ... is op du kahrt

Do you have a detailed map of the area?
Heeft u een gedetailleerde kaart van de omgeving?
hayft uu un CHu-day-tail-layr-du kahrt van du om-CHay-ving

Can you draw me a map?
Kunt u een kaart voor mij tekenen?
kunt uu un kahrt vohr mei tay-ku-nu

Do you have a guide book / leaflet in English?
Heeft u een gids / brochure in het Engels?
hayft uu un CHids / bro-shuu-ru in het eng-els

I'd like the English language version (of a cassette guide)
Ik wil graag de Engelse versie
ik wil CHrahCH du eng-el-su ver-see

Where can I buy an English newspaper?
Waar kan ik een Engelse krant kopen?
wahr kan ik un eng-el-su krant koh-pu

Do you have any English newspapers / books?
Heeft u Engelse kranten / boeken?
hayft uu un eng-el-su kran-tu / boo-ku

When do the English newspapers arrive?
Wanneer komen de Engelse kranten?
wan-nayr koh-mu du eng-el-su kran-tu

Reserve (name newspaper) **for me, please**
Bewaar de ... voor mij, alstublieft
bu-wahr du ... vohr mei als-tuu-bleeft

■ **DIRECTIONS** ■ **SIGHTSEEING & TOURIST OFFICE**

*The Dutch use the metric system. Note that a Dutch pound – **pond**
is 500 grams, and the Dutch ounce – **ons** is 100 grams.*

■ LIQUIDS

1/2 litre of... *(c.1 pint)*	halve liter...	**hal**-vu **lee**-ter...
a litre of...	een liter...	un **lee**-ter...
a bottle of...	een fles...	un fles...
a glass of...	een glas...	un CHlas...

■ WEIGHTS

100 grams of...	een ons...	un ons...
1/2 kilo of... *(500 g)*	een pond...	un pond...
a kilo of... *(1000 g)*	een kilo...	un **kee**-loh...

■ FOOD

a slice of...	een plak...	un plak...
a portion of...	een portie...	un **por**-tsee...
a dozen...	een dozijn...	un doh-**zein**...
a box of...	een doos...	un dohs...
a packet of... *(large)*	een pak...	un pak...
a packet of... *(small)*	een pakje...	un **pak**-yu...
a tin of...	een blik...	un blik...
a jar of...	een pot...	un pot...

■ MISCELLANEOUS

a third	een derde	un **der**-du
a quarter	een kwart	un kwart
ten per cent	tien procent	teen proh-**cent**
more...	meer...	mayr...
less...	minder...	**min**-der...
enough	genoeg	CHu-**nooCH**
double	dubbel	**dub**-bel
twice	twee keer	tway kayr
three times	drie keer	dree kayr

■ FOOD ■ SHOPPING

Like other forms of public transport, the metro uses
strippenkaarten which are valid for 10 journeys or more.

INGANG	ENTRANCE
UITGANG	WAY OUT / EXIT

Where is the nearest metro station?
Waar is het dichtstbijzijnde metrostation?
*wahr is het **diCHtst**-bei-zein-du **may**-troh-stah-shon*

How does the (ticket) machine work?
Hoe werkt de stempelautomaat?
*hoo werkt du **stem**-pel-ou-toh-maht*

I'm going to...
Ik ga naar...
*ik **CHah** nahr...*

How do I get to...?
Hoe kom ik in...?
hoo kom ik in...

Do I have to change?
Moet ik overstappen?
*moot ik **oh**-ver-stap-pu*

Which line is it for...?
Welke lijn gaat naar...?
***wel**-ku lein CHaht nahr...*

In which direction?
In welke richting?
*In **wel**-ku **riCH**-ting*

What is the next stop?
Wat is de volgende halte?
*wat is du **vol**-CHen-du **hal**-tu*

Excuse me!
Pardon!
*par-**don**!*

Let me through, please
Laat me erdoor, alstublieft
*laht mu er-**dohr** als-tuu-**bleeft***

I'm getting off here
Ik stap hier uit
ik stap heer uit

■ **BUS** ■ **TAXI**

*Banks are generally open 0900-1700 Monday to Friday.
Alternatively, you will find foreign currency exchanges in most
cities with extended opening hours.*

GELDAUTOMAAT	CASH DISPENSER
VOER UW PAS IN	INSERT YOUR CARD
TOETS UW PINCODE IN ·	ENTER YOUR PERSONAL NUMBER
GELDOPNAME	CASH WITHDRAWAL
UW VERZOEK IS IN BEHANDELING	WE ARE DEALING WITH YOUR REQUEST
EEN OGENBLIK GEDULD A.U.B.	PLEASE WAIT

Where can I change some money?
  Waar kan ik geld wisselen?
  *wahr kan ik CHeld **wis**-su-lu*

I want to change these traveller's cheques
  Ik wil deze travellercheques wisselen
  *ik wil **day**-ze **trah**-vel-ler-checks **wis**-su-lu*

When does the bank open?
  Wanneer gaat de bank open?
  *wan-**nayr** CHaht du bank **oh**-pu*

What time does the bank close?
  Hoe laat gaat de bank dicht?
  hoo laht CHaht de bank diCHt

Can I pay with traveller's cheques?
  Kan ik met travellercheques betalen?
  *kan ik met **trah**-vel-ler-checks be-**tah**-lu*

Can I use my credit card to get guilders?
  Kan ik mijn creditcard gebruiken om guldens te krijgen?
  *kan ik mein **cray**-dit-card CHu-**brui**-ku om **CHul**-dens tu **krei**-CHu*

Can I use my card with this cash dispenser?
  Kan ik mijn pas / card gebruiken in deze geldautomaat?
  *kan ik mein pas / card CHu-**brui**-ku in day-ze **CHeld**-ou-toh-maht*

■**PAYING**

Are there any good concerts on?
Zijn er goede concerten?
zein er **CHoo**-*du kon-**cer**-tu*

Where can I get tickets?
Waar kan ik kaartjes krijgen?
wahr kan ik **kahr**-*chus* **krei**-*CHu*

What sort of music do you like?
Van welke muziek houdt u?
van **wel**-*ku muu-**zeek** hout uu*

I like...
Ik hou van...
ik hou van...

Which is your favourite group?
Wat is uw favoriete groep?
*wat is uuw fah-vo-**ree**-tu* CHroop

Who is your favourite singer? (male/female)
Wie is uw favoriete zanger / zangeres?
*wee is uuw fah-vo-**ree**-tu* **zang**-*er* / **zang**-*e-res*

Can you play any musical instruments?
Kunt u een muziekinstrument bespelen?
*kunt uu un muu-**zeek**-in-struu-ment bu-**spay**-lu*

I play...	**the guitar**	**the piano**	**the clarinet**
Ik speel...	de gitaar	piano	klarinet
ik spayl...	*du* CHee-**tahr**	*pee-**ah**-noh*	*klah-ree-**net***

Have you been to any good concerts recently?
Bent u kort geleden nog naar een goed concert geweest?
bent uu kort CHu-**lay**-*du noch nahr un* CHood kon-**sert** CHu-**wayst**

Do you like opera?
Houdt u van opera?
hout uu van **oh**-*pe-rah*

Do you like reggae? (familiar)
Hou je van reggae?
*hou yu van reg-**gae***

Do you like pop music? (familiar)
Hou je van popmuziek?
*hou yu van pop-muu-**zeek***

■ **ENTERTAINMENT**

63

0	**nul**	*nul*	**1st**	**eerste**	
1	**één**	*ayn*		**ayr**-*stu*	
2	**twee**	*tway*	**2nd**	**tweede**	
3	**drie**	*dree*		**tway**-*du*	
4	**vier**	*veer*	**3rd**	**derde**	
5	**vijf**	*veif*		**der**-*du*	
6	**zes**	*zes*			
7	**zeven**	**zay**-*vu*	**4th**	**vierde**	
8	**acht**	*aCHt*		**veer**-*du*	
9	**negen**	**nay**-*CHu*	**5th**	**vijfde**	
10	**tien**	*teen*		**veif**-*du*	
11	**elf**	*elf*			
12	**twaalf**	*twahlf*	**6th**	**zesde**	
13	**dertien**	**der**-*teen*		**zes**-*du*	
14	**veertien**	**vayr**-*teen*	**7th**	**zevende**	
15	**vijftien**	**veif**-*teen*		**zay**-*vun-du*	
16	**zestien**	**zes**-*teen*	**8th**	**achtste**	
17	**zeventien**	**zay**-*vu-teen*		**aCHt**-*stu*	
18	**achttien**	**aCHt**-*teen*	**9th**	**negende**	
19	**negentien**	**nay**-*CHu-teen*		**nay**-*CHun-du*	
20	**twintig**	**twin**-*tiCH*	**10th**	**tiende**	
21	**éénentwintig**	**ayn**-*en-twin-tiCH*		**teen**-*du*	
22	**tweeëntwintig**	**tway**-*en-twin-tiCH*			
23	**drieëntwintig**	**dree**-*en-twin-tiCH*			
24	**vierentwintig**	**veer**-*en-twin-tiCH*			
25	**vijfentwintig**	**veif**-*en-twin-tiCH*			
26	**zesentwintig**	**zes**-*en-twin-tiCH*			
27	**zevenentwintig**	**zay**-*vu-en-twin-tiCH*			
28	**achtentwintig**	**aCHt**-*en-twin-tiCH*			
29	**negenentwintig**	**nay**-*CHu-en-twin-tiCH*			
30	**dertig**	**der**-*tiCH*			
40	**veertig**	**vayr**-*tiCH*			
50	**vijftig**	**veif**-*tich*			
60	**zestig**	**zes**-*tiCH*			
70	**zeventig**	**zay**-*vun-tiCH*			
80	**tachtig**	**taCH**-*tiCH*			
90	**negentig**	**nay**-*CHun-tiCH*			
100	**honderd**	**hon**-*derd*			
110	**honderdtien**	**hon**-*derd-teen*			
500	**vijfhonderd**	**veif**-*hon-derd*			
1,000	**duizend**	**dui**-*zend*			
2,000	**tweeduizend**	**tway**-*dui-zend*			
1 million	**één miljoen**	*ayn mil-***yoon**			

| AN APPOINTMENT | EEN AFSPRAAK |
| SWITCHBOARD | CENTRALE, DE |

I'd like to speak to the manager
Ik wil graag met de directeur spreken
*ik wil CHrahCH met du di-rek-**teur spray**-ku*

What is your address?
Wat is uw adres?
*wat is uuw **ah**-dres*

Which floor?
Welke verdieping?
***wel**-ku ver-**dee**-ping*

Can you photocopy this for me?
Kunt u dit voor mij fotokopiëren?
*kunt uu dit vohr mei **foh**-toh-koh-pee-ay-ru*

Do you use a courier service?
Gebruikt u een koeriersdienst?
*CHu-**bruikt** uu un koo-**reers**-deenst*

Can you send this for me?
Kunt u dit voor mij versturen?
*kunt uu dit vohr mei ver-**stuu**-ru*

What time does the office open / close?
Hoe laat gaat het kantoor open / dicht?
*hoo laht CHaht het kan-**tohr oh**-pu / diCHt*

How do I get to your office?
Hoe kom ik bij uw kantoor?
*hoo kom ik bei uuw kan-**tohr***

■ YOU MAY HEAR

Gaat u zitten, alstublieft ... komt zo bij u
*CHaht uu **zit**-tu als-tuu-**bleeft** ... komt zoh bei uu*
Please take a seat ... will be with you in just a moment

Een ogenblikje, alstublieft
*un **oh**-CHen-blik-yu als-tuu-**bleeft***
One moment please

■ BUSINESS–MEETING ■ FAX ■ LETTERS

TOTAL	TOTAAL, HET
BILL	REKENING, DE
CASH DESK	KASSA, DE
INVOICE	FAKTUUR, DE
PAY AT THE CASH DESK	BETAAL AAN DE KASSA
RECEIPT	KASSABON, DE

How much is it?
Hoeveel kost het?
hoo-vayl kost het

Can I pay...?   **by credit card**   **by cheque**
Kan ik betalen...?   per creditcard   met een cheque
*kan ik bu-**tah**-lu...*   *per **cre**-dit-card*   *met un check*

Do you take credit cards?
Accepteert u creditcards?
*ak-cep-**tayrt** uu **cre**-dit-cards*

Is service included?   **Is VAT included?**
Is de bediening inbegrepen?   Is het inclusief BTW?
*is du bu-**dee**-ning in-bu-**CHray**-pu*   *is het in-**cluu**-seef bay-tay-way*

Put it on my bill
Zet het maar op mijn rekening
*zet het mahr op mein **ray**-ku-ning*

I need a receipt
Ik heb een kassabon nodig
*ik heb un kas-**sah**-bon **noh**-diCH*

Do I pay in advance?   **Where do I pay?**
Moet ik vooruitbetalen?   Waar moet ik betalen?
*moot ik vohr-uit-bu-**tah**-lu*   *wahr moot ik bu-**tah**-lu*

I'm sorry   **I've nothing smaller**
Het spijt me   Ik heb niets kleiners
het speit mu   *ik heb neets **klei**-ners*

■ MONEY ■ SHOPPING

SUPER	**4 STAR**
LOODVRIJ	**UNLEADED**
DIESEL	**DIESEL**
BENZINE	**PETROL**
BENZINEPOMP	**PETROL PUMP**

Is there a petrol station near here?
Is er een benzinepomp in de buurt?
*is er un ben-**zee**-nu-pomp in du buurt*

Fill it up, please
Volmaken, alstublieft
*vol-**mah**-ku als-tuu-**bleeft***

Can you check the oil / water?
Kunt u olie / water controleren?
*Kunt uu **oh**-lee / **wah**-ter kon-**troh**-lay-ru*

...guilders worth of unleaded petrol, please
...gulden loodvrije benzine, alstublieft
*...**CHul**-du **lohd**-vrei-yu ben-**zee**-nu als-tuu-**bleeft***

Where is...?
Waar is...?
wahr is...

the air pump
de luchtpomp
*du **luCHt**-pomp*

the water
het water
*het **wah**-ter*

Can you check the tyre pressure, please?
Kunt u de spanning van de banden controleren, alstublieft?
*kunt uu du **span**-ning van de **ban**-du kon-**troh**-lay-ru als-tuu-**bleeft***

Fill this can with petrol, please
Vul dit blik met benzine, alstublieft
*vul dit blik met ben-**zee**-nu als-tuu-**bleeft***

Can I pay with this credit card?
Kan ik dit met deze creditcard betalen?
*kan ik dit met **day**-ze **cre**-dit-card bu-**tah**-lu*

■ **YOU MAY HEAR**

Welke pomp heeft u gebruikt?
*wel-ku pomp hayft uu CHu-**bruikt***
Which pump did you use?

■ **BREAKDOWNS** ■ **CAR**

67

DROGIST(ERIJ)	PHARMACY / CHEMIST
DIENSTDOENDE DROGIST	DUTY CHEMIST
RECEPT	PRESCRIPTION

I don't feel well
Ik voel me niet goed
ik vool mu neet CHood

Have you something for...?
Heeft u iets voor...?
hayft uu eets vohr...

a headache
hoofdpijn
hohfd-pein

car sickness
reisziekte
reis-zeek-tu

diarrhoea
diarree
dee-ar-ray

I have a rash
Ik heb uitslag
ik heb uit-slaCH

Is it safe for children?
Is het geschikt voor kinderen?
is het CHu-schikt vohr kin-du-ru

How much should I give?
Hoeveel moet ik geven?
hoo-vayl moot ik CHay-vu

■ **YOU MAY HEAR**

Driemaal daags voor / met / na maaltijden
dree-mahl dahCHs vohr / met / nah mahl-tei-du
Take it three times a day before / with / after meals

■ **WORDS YOU MAY NEED**

antiseptic	antisepticum, het	*an-tee-sep-teekum*
aspirin	aspirine, de	*as-pee-ree-nu*
condoms	condooms, de	*kon-dohms*
dental floss	dental floss, het	*den-tal floss*
plasters	pleisters, de	*pleis-ters*
sanitary pads	inlegkruisjes, de	*in-leCH-kruis-yus*
sanitary towels	maandverband, het	*mahnd-ver-band*
sore throat	zere keel, de	*zay-ru kayl*
tampons	tampons, de	*tam-pons*
toothpaste	tandpasta, de	*tand-pas-tah*

■ **BODY** ■ **DOCTOR**

Tapes for video cameras and camcorders can be bought in photography shops and department stores.

Where can I buy tapes for a video camera?
Waar kan ik een videoband voor mijn videocamera kopen?
*wahr kan ik un **vee**-day-oh-band vohr mein **vee**-day-oh-kah-may-rah **koh**-pu*

A colour film
Een kleurenfilm
*un **kleu**-ru-film*

with 24 / 36 exposures
met 24 / 36 opnamen
*met **veer**-en-twin-tiCH / **zes**-en-der-tiCH op-**nah**-mu*

A video tape for this video camera
Een videoband voor deze videocamera
*un **vee**-day-oh-band voor day-zu **vee**-day-oh-kah-may-rah*

Have you batteries...?
Heeft u batterijen...?
*hayft uu **bat**-tu-rei-yu...*

for this camera
voor deze camera
*vohr **day**-zu kah-may-rah*

Can you develop this film?
Kunt u deze film ontwikkelen?
*kunt uu **day**-ze film ont-**wik**-ku-lu*

How much will it be?
Hoeveel kost het?
hoo-vayl kost het

I'd like mat / glossy prints
Ik wil graag matte / glanzende afdrukken
*ik wil CHrahCH **mat**-tu / CHlan-zen-du af-**druk**-ku*

When will the photos be ready?
Wanneer zijn de foto's klaar?
*wan-**nayr** zein du **foh**-tohs klahr*

The film is stuck
De film zit vast
du film zit vast

Can you take it out for me?
Kunt u hem er voor mij uithalen?
*kunt uu hem er vohr mei uit-**hah**-lu*

Is it OK to take pictures here?
Mag ik hier foto's maken?
*maCH ik heer **foh**-tohs **mah**-ku*

Would you take a picture of us, please?
Wilt u een foto van ons maken, alstublieft?
*wilt uu un **foh**-toh van ons **mah**-ku als-tuu-**bleeft***

■ SHOPPING

Main post offices are open Mon.-Fri. (0900-1700) and Saturday mornings.

POST OFFICE	POSTKANTOOR, HET
POSTBOX	BRIEVENBUS, DE
PO BOX	POSTBUS, DE
STAMPS	POSTZEGELS, DE

Is there a post office near here?
Is er een postkantoor in de buurt?
*is er un **post**-kan-tohr in du buurt*

Which counter sells stamps?
Aan welk loket worden postzegels verkocht?
*ahn welk loh-**ket** wor-du **post**-zay-CHels ver-**koCHt***

Can I have stamps for ... postcards to Great Britain?
Mag ik postzegels voor ... briefkaarten naar Groot Brittannië?
*maCH ik **post**-zay-CHels vohr...**breef**-kahr-tu nahr CHroht **Brit**-tan-nee-yu*

I want to send this letter registered post
Ik wil deze brief aangetekend versturen
*ik wil **day**-zu breef **ahn**-CHu-tay-kend ver-**stuu**-ru*

How much is it to send this parcel?
Hoeveel kost het om dit pakje te versturen?
***hoo**-vayl kost het om dit **pak**-yu tu ver-**stuu**-ru*

by air
per luchtpost
*per **luCHt**-post*

It's a gift
Het is een cadeau
*het is un kah-**doh***

The value of contents is ... guilders
De waarde van de inhoud is ... gulden
*du **wahr**-du van du **in**-houd is ... **CHul**-du*

■ YOU MAY HEAR

Vul dit formulier in
*vul dit for-muu-**lier** in*
Fill in this form

Can you help me?
Kunt u mij helpen?
kunt uu mei hel-pu

I only speak a little Dutch
Ik spreek slechts een beetje Nederlands
ik sprayk sleCHts un bay-chu nay-der-lands

Does anyone here speak English?
Spreekt hier iemand Engels?
spraykt heer ee-mand eng-els

What's the matter?
Wat is er aan de hand?
wat is er ahn du hand

I would like to speak to whoever is in charge
Ik wil graag met de chef spreken
ik wil CHrahCH met du shef spray-ku

I'm lost
Ik ben verdwaald
ik ben ver-dwahld

How do I get to...?
Hoe kom ik bij...?
hoo kom ik bei...

I've missed my...	**train**	**plane**	**connection**	**bus**
Ik miste mijn...	trein	vliegtuig	verbinding	bus
ik mis-tu mein...	*trein*	*vleeCH-tuiCH*	*ver-bin-ding*	*bus*

The coach has left without me / us
De bus is zonder mij / ons vertrokken
du bus is zon-der mei / ons ver-trok-ku

Can you show me how this works?
Kunt u mij laten zien hoe dit werkt?
kunt uu mei lah-tu zeen hoo dit werkt

I have lost my purse
Ik heb mijn portemonnaie verloren
ik heb mein por-tu-mon-nay ver-lo-ru

I need to get to...
Ik moet naar...
ik moot nahr...

Leave me alone!
Laat me met rust!
laht mu met rust!

Go away!
Ga weg
CHah weCH

■ COMPLAINTS ■ EMERGENCIES

Do you have...?
Heeft u...?
hayft uu...

When...?
Wanneer...?
wan-nayr...

At what time...?
Hoe laat...?
hoo laht...

Where is / are...?
Waar is / zijn...?
wahr is / zein...

Can I...?
Kan ik...?
kan ik...

May we...?
Mogen wij...?
moh-CHu wei...

Is it...?
Is het...?
is het...

Are they...?
Zijn zij...?
zein zei...

Is / Are there...?
Is / Zijn er...?
is / zein er...

Is it far?
Is het ver?
is het ver

What time is it?
Hoe laat is het?
hoo laht is het

Who are you?
Wie bent u?
wee bent uu

Who...?
Wie...?
wee...

What...?
Wat...?
wat...

Why...?
Waarom...?
wahr-om...

How many...?
Hoeveel...?
hoo-vayl...

How much is it?
Hoeveel is het?
hoo-vayl is het

How...?
Hoe...?
hoo...

Which one?
Welke?
wel-ku

Where are the toilets?
Waar zijn de toiletten?
wahr zein du twa-let-tu

SCHOENMAKER	SHOE REPAIR SHOP
KLAAR TERWIJL U WACHT	REPAIRS WHILE YOU WAIT

This is broken
Het is kapot
*het is kah-**pot***

Where can I get this repaired?
Waar kan ik dit laten repareren?
*wahr kan ik dit **lah**-tu ray-pah-**ray**-ru*

Is it worth repairing?
Is reparatie de moeite waard?
*is ray-pah-**rah**-tsee du **mooee**-tu wahrd*

Repair...	**these shoes**	**my watch**
Repareer...	deze schoenen	mijn horloge
*ray-pah-**rayr**...*	*day-zu **schoo**-nu*	*mein hor-**loh**-shu*

How much will it be?
Hoeveel kost het?
***hoo**-vayl kost het*

Can you do it straightaway?
Kunt u het direct doen?
*kunt uu het **dee**-rekt doon*

How long will it take?
Hoe lang duurt het?
hoo lang duurt het

When will it be ready?
Wanneer is het klaar?
*wan-**nayr** is het klahr*

Where can I have my shoes reheeled?
Waar kan ik nieuwe hakken op mijn schoenen laten zetten?
*wahr kan ik **nee**-wu **hak**-ku op mein **schoo**-nu **lah**-tu **zet**-tu*

I need some...	**glue**	**Sellotape®**
Ik heb nodig...	lijm	plakband
*ik heb **noh**-diCH...*	*leim*	***plak**-band*

a light bulb	**an electrical fuse**
een gloeilamp	een zekering
*un **CHlooee**-lamp*	*un **zay**-ku-ring*

Do you have a needle and thread?
Heeft u naald en draad?
hayft uu nahld en drahd

■ BREAKDOWNS

Come in!
Kom binnen!
*kom **bin**-nu*

Come back later, please
Kom straks terug, alstublieft
*kom straks tu-**ruCH** als-tuu-**bleeft***

I'd like breakfast in my room
Ik wil graag ontbijt op mijn kamer
*ik wil CHrahCH ont-**beit** op mein **kah**-mer*

Please bring me...
Alstublieft, breng me...
*als-tuu-**bleeft** breng mu...*

a glass
een glas
un CHlas

clean towels
schone badhandoeken
***schoh**-nu **bad**-hand-doo-ku*

toilet paper
toiletpapier
*twa-**let**-pah-peer*

I'd like an early morning call tomorrow
Ik wil 's morgens graag gewekt worden
*ik wil **smor**-CHuns CHrahCH CHu-**wekt wor**-du*

at 6 o'clock
om 6 uur
om zes uur

at 6.30
om 6.30
*om half **zay**-vu*

at 7 o'clock
om 7 uur
*om **zay**-vu uur*

I'd like an outside line
Ik wil graag een buitenlijn
*Ik wil CHrahCH un **bui**-tu-lein*

The ... doesn't work
De/Het ... werkt niet
du/het ... werkt neet

Can you repair it, please?
Kunt u het repareren, alstublieft?
*kunt uu het ray-pah-**ray**-ru als-tuu-**bleeft***

I need more coat hangers
Ik heb meer kleerhangers nodig
*ik heb mayr **klayr**-hang-ers **noh**-diCH*

Do you have a laundry service?
Heeft u een wasserij?
*hayft uu un **was**-su-rei*

■ HOTEL ■ LAUNDRY ■ TELEPHONE

UITVERKOOP	SALE / REDUCTIONS
OPEN TOT...	OPEN TODAY TILL...

How do I get to the shopping area?
Hoe kom ik bij het winkelcentrum?
*hoo kom ik bei het **win**-kel-cen-trum*

I'm looking for a present for...
Ik zoek een cadeau voor...
*ik zook un kah-**doh** voor...*

my mother	a child
mijn moeder	een kind
*mein **moo**-der*	*un kind*

Where do they sell...?
Waar verkopen ze...?
*wahr ver-**koh**-pu zu...*

toys	gifts
speelgoed	cadeautjes
spayl-CHood	*kah-**doh**-chus*

Can you recommend any good shops?
Kunt u een goede winkel aanbevelen?
*kunt uu un **CHoo**-du **win**-kel **ahn**-bu-vay-lu*

Which floor is the shoe department on?
Op welke verdieping is de schoenenafdeling?
*op **wel**-ku ver-**dee**-ping is du **schoo**-nu-af-day-ling*

I'd like something similar to this
Ik wil graag iets wat hier op lijkt
ik wil CHrahCH eets wat heer op leikt

It's too expensive for me
Het is te duur voor mij
hot is tu duur vohr mei

Have you anything else?
Heeft u iets anders?
*hayft uu eets **an**-ders*

Is there a market?
Is er een markt?
is er un markt

On which day?
Op welke dag?
*op **wel**-ku daCH*

■ YOU MAY HEAR

Kan ik u helpen?
*kan ik uu **hel**-pu*
Can I help you?

Anders nog iets?
***an**-ders noCH eets*
Would you like anything else?

■ CLOTHES ■ MEASUREMENTS & QUANTITIES ■ SHOPS

Some shops close for lunch approx. 1230-1330. Department stores remain open all day. During the week most shops shut for at least half a day. The actual closing day differs from town to town.

baker's	BAKKER	**bak**-ker
bookshop	BOEKHANDEL	**book**-han-del
butcher's	SLAGER	**slah**-CHer
cake shop	BANKETBAKKER	ban-**ket**-bak-ker
clothes (women's)	DAMESMODE	**dah**-mes-moh-du
clothes (men's)	HERENMODE	**hay**-ru-moh-du
clothes (children's)	KINDERKLEDING	**kin**-der-klay-ding
dry-cleaner's	STOMERIJ	**stoh**-mu-rei
electrical goods	ELEKTRISCHE ARTIKELEN	**ay**-lek-tri-su ar-**tee**-ku-lu
fishmonger's	VISHANDEL	**vis**-han-del
furniture	MEUBELEN	**meu**-bu-lu
gifts	CADEAUS	kah-**dohs**
greengrocer's	GROENTEBOER	**CHroon**-tu-boor
grocer's	KRUIDENIER	krui-du-**neer**
hairdresser's	KAPPER	**kap**-per
ironmonger's	IJZERWAREN	**ei**-zer-wah-ru
jeweller's	JUWELIER	**yuu**-wu-leer
market	MARKT	markt
pharmacy	DROGIST	**droh**-CHist
self-service	ZELFBEDIENING	**zelf**-bu-dee-ning
shoe shop	SCHOENENWINKEL	**schoo**-nu-win-kel
shop	WINKEL	**win**-kel
sports shop	SPORTZAAK	**sport**-zahk
stationer's	KANTOORBOEKHANDEL	kan-**tohr**-book-han-del
supermarket	SUPERMARKT	**suu**-per-markt
sweet shop	SNOEPWINKEL	**snoop**-win-kel
tobacconist's	SIGARENHANDEL	**see**-gah-ru-han-del
toy shop	SPEELGOEDWINKEL	**spayl**-CHood-win-kel

*The tourist office is called **VVV** or **Tourist Information**. If you are looking for somewhere to stay they should have details of hotels, campsites, etc. In addition they supply information on local events and entertainment.*

Where is the tourist office?
Waar is het VVV kantoor?
*wahr is het vay-vay-vay kan-**tohr***

What can we visit in the area?
Wat kunnen we bezoeken?
*wat **kun**-nu wu bu-**zoo**-ku*

Have you any leaflets?
Heeft u brochures?
*hayft uu bro-**shuu**-res*

When can we visit the...?
Wanneer kunnen we de/het ... bezoeken?
*wan-**nayr kun**-nu wu du/het ... bu-**zoo**-ku*

We'd like to go to...
Wij willen graag naar...
*wei **wil**-lu CHrahCH nahr...*

Are there any excursions?
Zijn er excursies?
*zein er ex-**cur**-sees*

When does it leave?
Hoe laat begint het?
*hoo laht bu-**CHint** het*

Where does it leave from?
Waar begint het?
*wahr be-**CHint** het*

How much does it cost to get in?
Hoeveel kost het om naar binnen te komen?
***hoo**-vayl kost het om nahr **bin**-nu tu **koh**-mu*

Are there any reductions for...?
Is er korting voor...?
*is er **kor**-ting vohr...*

children	students	unemployed	senior citizens
kinderen	studenten	werklozen	65+ers
***kin**-du-ru*	***stuu**-den-tu*	*werk-**loh**-zu*	***veif**-en-zes-tlg-plus-sers*

■ ENTERTAINMENT ■ MAPS, GUIDES & NEWSPAPERS

SIGNS & NOTICES ——————— ENGLISH-DUTCH

BAGAGE
LEFT LUGGAGE

BEGANE GROND
GROUND FLOOR

BETAAL AAN DE KASSA
PAY AT THE CASH DESK

BEZET
ENGAGED

BUITEN DIENST
OUT OF ORDER

DAMES
LADIES

DATUM
DATE

DUWEN
PUSH

GEEN INGANG
NO ENTRY

GESLOTEN
CLOSED

HEET
HOT

HEREN
GENTS

INGANG
ENTRANCE

INFORMATIE
INFORMATION

KAARTVERKOOP
TICKET OFFICE

KAMERS VRIJ
VACANCIES

KASSA
CASH DESK

KELDER
BASEMENT

KOUD
COLD

LIFT
LIFT

NIET AANRAKEN
DO NOT TOUCH

NIET OP HET IJS
DO NOT STEP ON THE ICE

NIET ROKEN ALSTUBLIEFT
NO SMOKING PLEASE

NOODUITGANG
EMERGENCY EXIT

ONGEVALLEN
CASUALTY DEPT.

OPEN
OPEN

PRIVÉ
PRIVATE

ROKEN
SMOKING

SPOOR/PERRON
PLATFORM (train)

TE HUUR
FOR HIRE, TO RENT

TE KOOP
FOR SALE

TOILETTEN
TOILETS

TREKKEN
PULL

VERKOOP
SALES

VOL
NO VACANCIES

VRIJ
FREE, VACANT

UITVERKOOP
SALE

UITGANG
EXIT

ZELFBEDIENING
SELF-SERVICE

WARM
WARM

ZWEMMEN GEVAARLIJK
SWIMMING DANGEROUS

ZWEMMEN VERBODEN
NO BATHING

78

Where can I...?
Waar kan ik...?
wahr kan ik...

play tennis	**play golf**
tennissen	golfen
ten-*nis*-su	**CHol**-fu

go swimming	**go jogging**	**skate**
zwemmen	joggen	schaatsen
zwem-mu	**dshoCH**-CHu	**schaht**-su

How much is it per hour?
Hoeveel kost het per uur?
hoo-vayl kost het per uur

Do you have to be a member?
Moet je lid zijn?
moot yu lid zein

Can I hire...?	**rackets**	**golf clubs**	**skates**
Kan ik ... huren?	rackets	golfclubs	schaatsen
kan ik ... **huu**-ru	ra-**kets**	**CHolf**-clubs	**schaht**-su

We'd like to go to see *(name team)* **play**
Wij willen graag ... zien spelen
*wei **wil**-lu CHrahCH ... zeen **spay**-lu*

I like...	**sailing**	**surfing**
Ik hou van...	zeilen	surfen
ik hou van	**zei**-lu	**sur**-fu

I like walking	**Are there any special walking routes?**
Ik hou van wandelen	Zijn er speciale wandelroutes?
*ik hou van **wan**-du-lu*	*zein er **spay**-cee-ah-lu **wan**-del-roo-tes*

What sports...?*(familiar)*	**do you play**	**do you like to watch**
Welke sporten...?	speel je	zie je graag
wel-ku **spor**-tu...	*spayl yu*	*zee yu CHrahCH*

I do not like sport
Ik hou niet van sport
ik hou neet van sport

■ **LEISURE/INTERESTS** ■ **SKIING** ■ **WALKING**

All these items can be bought at the stationer's – kantoorboekhandel.

biro	balpen, de	**bal**-pen
book	boek, het	book
card (greetings)	briefkaart, de	**breef**-kahrt
cardboard	karton, het	kar-**ton**
crayons (wax)	waskrijtjes, de	**was**-krei-chus
envelopes	enveloppen, de	en-vu-**lop**-pu
exercise book	oefenboek, het	**oo**-fen-book
felt-tip pen	viltstift, de	**vilt**-stift
folder	map, de	map
glue	lijm, de	leim
ink	inkt, de	inkt
ink cartridge	inktpatroon, het	**inkt**-pah-trohn
magazine	tijdschrift, het	**teid**-schrift
newspaper	krant, de	krant
note pad	notitieblok, het	noh-**tee**-tee-blok
paint	verf, de	verf
paper	papier, het	pah-**peer**
paperback	paperback, de	**pay**-per-bek
paperclip	paperclip, de	**pay**-per-klip
pen	pen, de	pen
pencil	potlood, het	**pot**-lohd
pencil sharpener	puntenslijper, de	**pun**-tu-slei-per
rubber	gum, het	CHum
ruler	liniaal, de	lee-nee-**ahl**
Sellotape®	plakband, de	**plak**-band
sheet of paper	vel papier, het	vel **pah**-peer
stapler	nietmachine, de	**neet**-mah-shee-nu
staples	nietjes, de	**nee**-chus
writing paper	schrijfpapier, het	**schreif**-pah-peer

I need a taxi
Ik heb een taxi nodig
*ik heb un tak-**see** noh-diCH*

Where is the taxi rank?
Waar is de taxistandplaats?
*wahr is du tak-**see**-stand-plahts*

Please order me a taxi
Wilt u alstublieft een taxi bestellen
*wilt uu als-tuu-**bleeft** un tak-**see** bu-**stel**-lu*

straightaway for (time)
direct   voor...
*dee-**rekt***   *vohr...*

How much will the taxi cost to...?
Hoeveel kost de taxi naar...?
***hoo**-vayl kost du tak-**see** nahr...*

the centre
het centrum
*het cen-**trum***

the station
het station
*het stah-**shon***

the airport
het vliegveld
*het **vlieCH**-veld*

this address
dit adres
*dit ah-**dres***

Please take me / us to...
Breng mij / ons alstublieft naar...
*breng mei / ons als-tuu-**bleeft** nahr...*

How much is it?
Hoeveel is het?
***hoo**-vayl is het*

Why are you charging me so much?
Waarom vraagt u zoveel?
*wahr-**om** vrahCHt uu zoh-**vayl***

That is more than on the meter
Dat is meer dan op de meter
*dat is mayr dan op du **may**-ter*

Keep the change
Laat zo maar zitten
*laht zoh mahr **zit**-tu*

Sorry, I don't have any change
Sorry, ik heb geen kleingeld
*sor-**ree** ik heb CHayn **klein**-CHeld*

I'm in a hurry
Ik heb haast
ik heb hahst

Is it far?
Is het ver?
is het ver

I have to catch the ... o'clock flight / train to...
Ik moet de vlucht / trein van ... uur naar ... halen
*ik moot de vluCHt van ... uur nahr ... **hah**-lu*

■ OFFICE ■ SHOPPING

81

To phone the Netherlands from the UK, the international code is
00 31 *plus the Dutch area code (e.g. Amsterdam* **20**,
Rotterdam **10**, *The Hague* **70**) *followed by the number you require.*
To phone the UK from the Netherlands, dial **00 44** *plus the UK*
area code less the first **0**, *e.g., London (0)***171** *or (0)***181**.

PHONECARD	**TELEFOONKAART, DE**
TELEPHONE DIRECTORY	**TELEFOONBOEK, HET**
YELLOW PAGES	**GOUDEN GIDS, DE**
ANSWERING MACHINE	**ANTWOORDAPPARAAT, HET**
DIAL THE NUMBER	**DRAAI HET NUMMER**
TO PICK UP / TO HANG UP	**OPNEMEN / OPHANGEN**

I want to make a phone call
Ik wil opbellen
ik wil **op**-bel-lu

What coins do I need?
Welke munten heb ik nodig?
wel-ku **mun**-tu heb ik **noh**-diCH

Can you show me how this phone works?
Kunt u mij laten zien hoe deze telefoon werkt?
kunt uu mei **lah**-tu zeen hoo **day**-zu tay-lu-**fohn** werkt

Where can I buy a phonecard?
Waar kan ik een telefoonkaart kopen?
*wahr kan ik un tay-lu-***fohn**-*kahrt* **koh**-pu

Mr Smit, please
Meneer Smit, alstublieft
*mu-***nayr** *Smit als-tuu-***bleeft**

Extension number...
Toestelnummer...
too-stel-num-mer...

Can I speak to...?
Mag ik...?
maCH ik...

I would like to speak to...
Ik wil graag ... spreken
ik wil CHrahCH ... **spray**-ku

This is Jim Brown
Dit is Jim Brown
dit is Jim Brown

Speaking
Daar spreekt u mee
dahr spraykt uu may

Can I have an outside line?
Mag ik een buitenlijn?
*maCH ik un **bui**-tu-lein*

I'll call back later / tomorrow
Ik bel later / morgen terug
*ik bel **lah**-ter / **mor**-Chu tu-**ruCH***

We were cut off
Wij werden afgesneden
*wei **wer**-du af-CHu-**snay**-du*

There is no reply
Er wordt niet opgenomen
*er wordt neet op-CHu-**noh**-mu*

■ **YOU MAY HEAR**

Hallo
*hal-**lo***
Hello

Met wie spreek ik?
met wee sprayk ik
Who am I talking to?

Met wie wilt u spreken?
*met wee wilt uu **spray**-ku*
Who do you wish to talk to?

Een ogenblik
*un **oh**-CHu-blik*
Just a moment

Blijf aan de lijn, alstublieft
*bleif ahn du lein als-tuu-**bleeft***
Hold on, please

Hij/Zij komt er aan
hei/zei komt er ahn
He/She is coming

De lijn is bezet
*du lein is bu-**zet***
It's engaged

Kunt u later terugbellen?
*kunt uu **lah**-ter tu-**ruCH**-bel-lu*
Can you try again later?

Wilt u een boodschap achterlaten?
*wilt uu un **bohd**-schap aCH-ter-**lah**-tu*
Do you want to leave a message?

U heeft het verkeerde nummer
*uu hayft het ver-**kayr**-du **num**-mer*
You've got a wrong number

Dit is het antwoordapparaat van…
*dit is het **ant**-wohrd-ap-pah-raht van…*
This is the answering machine of…

Spreek alstublieft uw boodschap in na de toon…
*sprayk als-tuu-**bleeft** uuw **bohd**-schap in nah du tohn*
Please leave a message after the tone

■ **BUSINESS–MEETING** ■ **FAX** ■ **OFFICE**

REMOTE CONTROL	AFSTANDSBEDIENING, DE
SERIES	SERIE, DE
VIDEO RECORDER	VIDEO, DE
NEWS	NIEUWS, HET
TO SWITCH ON	AANZETTEN
TO SWITCH OFF	AFZETTEN
PROGRAMME	PROGRAMMA, HET
CARTOONS	TEKENFILMS, DE

Where is the television?
Waar is de televisie?
wahr is du tay-lu-vee-see

How do you switch it on?
Hoe gaat hij aan?
hoo CHaht hei ahn

Which button do I press?
Welke knop moet ik indrukken?
wel-ku knop moot ik in-druk-ku

Could you lower the volume please?
Kunt u het geluid wat zachter zetten, alstublieft?
kunt uu het CHu-luid wat zaCH-ter zet-tu als-tuu-bleeft

May I turn the volume up?
Mag ik het geluid harder zetten?
maCH ik het CHu-luid har-der zet-tu

What's on television?
Wat is er op televisie?
wat is er op tay-lu-vee-see

When is the news?
Hoe laat komt het nieuws?
hoo laht komt het neews

Do you have any English-speaking channels?
Heeft u Engels-talige kanalen?
hayft u eng-els-tah-li-CHu kah-nah-lu

When are the children's programmes?
Wanneer komen de kinderprogramma's?
wan-nayr koh-mu du kin-der-proh-CHram-mahs

Do you have any English videos?
Heeft u Engels-talige video's?
hayft uu eng-els-tah-li-CHu vee-day-ohs

PLAY	TONEELSTUK, HET
STALLS	STALLES, DE
CIRCLE	BALKON, HET
UPPER CIRCLE	TWEEDE BALKON, HET
SEAT	ZITPLAATS, DE
CLOAKROOM	KLEEDKAMER, DE

What's on at the theatre?
Wat speelt er in het theater?
*wat spaylt er in het tay-**ah**-ter*

How do we get to *(name)*...?
Hoe komen we bij...?
*hoe **koh**-mu wu bei...*

What prices are the tickets?
Hoeveel kosten de kaartjes?
***hoo**-vayl **kos**-tu du **kahr**-chus*

I'd like two tickets...
Ik wil graag twee kaartjes...
*ik wil CHrahCH tway **kahr**-chus...*

for tonight
voor vanavond
*vohr van-**ah**-vond*

for tomorrow night
voor morgenavond
*vohr mor-CHu-**ah**-vond*

for 5th August
voor 5 augustus
*vohr veif ou-**CHus**-tus*

in the stalls
stalles
stal-lus

in the circle
balkon
*bal-**kon***

in the upper circle
tweede balkon
tway**-du bal-**kon

How long is the interval?
Hoe lang duurt de pauze?
*hoo lang duurt du **pou**-zu*

Is there a bar?
Is er een bar?
is er un bar

When does the performance begin / end?
Hoe laat begint / eindigt de voorstelling?
*hoo laht be-**CHint** / **ein**-diCHt du **vohr**-stel-ling*

I enjoyed the play
Ik heb genoten van het toneelstuk
*ik heb CHu-**noh**-tu van het toh-**nayl**-stuk*

It was very good
Het was erg goed
het was erCH CHood

■ ENTERTAINMENT ■ LEISURE/INTERESTS

> The Dutch use the 24-hour clock as follows when they speak.
> After **1200** midday, it continues: **1300** – één uur, **1400** – twee
> **uur**, etc. However, announcements, as in railway stations, and
> written notices use the 24-hour clock properly.
> Note that 9.30 in Dutch is **half tien**, literally meaning **half ten**.

What time is it?	**am**	**pm**
Hoe laat is het?	voormiddag	namiddag
hoo laht is het	*vohr-**mid**-daCH*	*nah-**mid**-daCH*

It's...	**2 o'clock**	**3 o'clock**	**6 o'clock** (etc.)
Het is...	2 uur	3 uur	6 uur
het is...	*tway uur*	*dree uur*	*zes uur*

It's 1 o'clock	**It's 1200 midday**	**At midnight**
Het is 1 uur	het is 12 uur 's middags	Middernacht
het is ayn uur	*het is twahlf uur **smid**-daCHs*	*mid-der-**naCHt***

9	9 uur
	nay-CHu uur
9.10	10 over 9
	*teen **oh**-ver **nay**-CHu*
quarter past 9	kwart over 9
	*kwart **oh**-ver **nay**-CHu*
9.20	10 voor half 10
	teen vohr half teen
9.30	half 10
	half teen
9.35	5 over half 10
	*veif **oh**-ver half teen*
quarter to 10	kwart voor 10
	kwart vohr teen
10 to 10	10 voor 10
	teen vohr teen

■ **NUMBERS**

When does it open / close?
Hoe laat gaat het open / dicht?
*hoo laht CHaht het **oh**-pu / diCHt*

When does it begin / finish?
Hoe laat begint / eindigt het?
*hoo laht bu-**CHint** / **ein**-diCHt het*

at 3 o'clock
om 3 uur
om dree uur

before 3 o'clock
voor 3 uur
vohr dree uur

after 3 o'clock
na 3 uur
nah dree uur

today
vandaag
***van**-dahCH*

tonight
vanavond
*van-**ah**-vond*

tomorrow
morgen
***mor**-CHu*

yesterday
gisteren
***CHis**-tu-ru*

the day before yesterday
eergisteren
***ayr**-CHis-tu-ru*

the day after tomorrow
overmorgen
***oh**-ver-mor-CHu*

in the morning
's morgens
***smor**-Chens*

this morning
vanmorgen
*van-**mor**-CHu*

this afternoon
vanmiddag
*van-**mid**-daCH*

in the evening
's avonds
***sah**-vonds*

this evening
vanavond
*van-**ah**-vond*

in the night
's nachts
snaCHts

this night
vannacht
*van-**naCHt***

at half past 7
om half 8
om half aCHt

at about 10 o'clock
om ongeveer 10 uur
*om on-CHu-**veer** teen uur*

in an hour's time
over een uur
***oh**-ver un uur*

in a little while
over een poosje
***oh**, ver un **poh**-shu*

two hours ago
twee uur geleden
*tway uur CHu-**lay**-du*

soon
gauw
CHouw

early
vroeg
vrooCH

late
laat
laht

later
later
***lah**-ter*

I'll do it...
Ik doe het...
ik doo het...

as soon as possible
zo gauw mogelijk
*zoh gouw **moh**-CHu-luk*

...at the latest
op z'n laatst...
op zun lahtst...

Dutch trains have two types of compartments: 1st class and 2nd class, both with smoking and non-smoking divisions.

NS	DUTCH NATIONAL RAILWAYS
(Nederlandse Spoorwegen)	
INTERCITY	INTERCITY
SNELTREIN	FAST TRAIN
STOPTREIN	SLOW TRAIN
TOESLAG	SUPPLEMENT PAYABLE
PERRON / SPOOR	PLATFORM

When is the next train to...?
Hoe laat vertrekt de volgende trein naar...?
*hoo laht ver-**trekt** du **vol**-CHen-du trein nahr...*

Two return tickets to...
Twee retour naar...
*tway ru-**toor** nahr...*

A single to...
Een enkeltje naar...
*un **en**-kel-chu nahr...*

1st / 2nd class
Eerste / Tweede klas
***ayr**-stu / **tway**-du klas*

Smoking
Roken
***roh**-ku*

Non smoking
Niet roken
*neet **roh**-ku*

Is there a supplement to pay?
Is er een toeslag?
*is er un **too**-slaCH*

I want to book a seat on the international train to...
Ik wil een plaats reserveren op de internationale trein naar...
*ik wil un plahts ray-ser-**vay**-ru op du in-ter-na-tee-oh-**nah**-le trein nahr...*

When is the first / last train to...?
Hoe laat vertrekt de eerste / laatste trein naar...?
*hoo laht ver-**trekt** de **ayr**-stu / **laht**-stu trein nahr...*

When does it arrive in...?
Hoe laat komt hij aan in...?
hoo laht komt hei ahn in...

Do I have to change?
Moet ik overstappen?
*moot ik **oh**-ver-stap-pu*

Where?
Waar?
wahr

How long is there to get the connection?
Hoe lang heb ik om over te stappen?
hoo lang heb ik om oh-ver tu stap-pu

Which platform does it leave from?
Van welk spoor vertrekt de trein?
van welk spohr ver-trekt du trein

Is this the right platform for the train to...?
Is dit het goede perron voor de trein naar...?
is dit het CHoo-du per-ron vohr du trein nahr...

Is this the train for...?
Gaat deze trein naar...?
CHaht day-zu trein nahr...

When will it leave?
Hoe laat vertrekt hij?
hoo laht ver-trekt hei

Why is the train delayed?
Waarom heeft de trein vertraging?
wahr-om hayft de trein ver-trah-CHing

Does the train stop at...?
Stopt de trein in...?
stopt du trein in...

Could you let me know when we get to...
Kunt u mij waarschuwen wanneer wij aankomen in...
kunt uu mei wahr-schuu-wu wan-nayr wei ahn-koh-mu in...

Is there a buffet on the train?
Is er een restauratie in de trein?
Is er un res-tou-rah-tsee in du trein

Is this seat free?
Is deze plaats vrij?
is day-zu plahts vrei

Excuse me
Pardon
par-don

■ **YOU MAY HEAR**

De intercity naar ..., staat gereed op spoor...
du in-ter-ci-tee nahr ... staht CHu-rayd op spohr...
The intercity train to ..., is now ready on platform...

■ **LUGGAGE**

Most Dutch restaurants will have vegetarian dishes. In addition there are vegetarian and special health food restaurants serving food without chemical additives.

Are there any vegetarian restaurants here?
Zijn er hier vegetarische restaurants?
*zein er heer vay-CHu-**tah**-ree-su res-tou-**rants***

Do you have any vegetarian dishes?
Heeft u vegetarische gerechten?
*hayft uu vay-CHu-**tah**-ree-su CHu-**reCH**-tu*

Which dishes have no meat / fish?
Welke gerechten bevatten geen vlees / vis?
***wel**-ku CHu-**reCH**-tu bu-**vat**-tu CHayn vlays / vis*

What fish dishes do you have?
Wat voor visgerechten heeft u?
*wat vohr vis-CHu-**reCH**-tu hayft uu*

I don't like meat
Ik hou niet van vlees
ik hou neet van vlays

What do you recommend?
Wat kunt u aanbevelen?
*wat kunt uu ahn-bu-**vay**-lu*

Is it made with vegetable stock?
Is het gemaakt met vegetarische bouillon?
*is het CHu-**mahkt** met vay-CHu-**tah**-ree-su bool-**yon***

Which dishes contain...?	**milk**	**butter**
Welke gerechten bevatten...?	melk	boter
*wel-ku CHu-**reCH**-tu bu-vat-tu...*	*melk*	***boh**-ter*

cheese	**eggs**	**chemical additives**
kaas	eieren	chemische toevoegingen
kahs	***ei**-yu-ru*	*CHay-mee-su **too**-voo-CHing-u*

■ **EATING OUT**

Are there any guided walks?
Zijn er wandeltochten met gidsen?
*zein er **wan**-del-toCH-tu met **CHid**-su*

Are there any special walking routes?
Zijn er speciale wandelroutes?
*zein er spay-cee-**ah**-le **wan**-del-roo-tus*

Do you have details?
Heeft u bijzonderheden?
*hayft u bee-**zon**-der-hay-du*

Do you have a guide to local walks?
Heeft u een gids met plaatselijke wandelingen?
*hayft uu un CHids met **plaht**-su-lu-ku **wan**-du-ling-u*

How many kilometres is the walk?
Hoeveel kilometer is de wandeling?
*hoo-vayl kee-loh-may-ter is du **wan**-du-ling*

How long will it take?
Hoe lang duurt het?
hoo lang duurt het

We'd like to come along
Wij willen graag meegaan
*wei **wil**-lu CHrahCH **may**-CHahn*

Do we need special clothing?
Hebben we speciale kleding nodig?
***heb**-bu wu spay-cee-**ah**-lu **klay**-ding **noh**-diCH*

Should we take...?
Moeten we ... meenemen?
***moo**-tu wu ... **may**-nay-mu*

water	food
water	voedsel
***wah**-ter*	***vood**-sel*

waterproofs	a compass	boots
regenkleding	een kompas	laarzen
***ray**-CHu-klay-ding*	*un kom-**pas***	***lahr**-zu*

What time does it get dark?
Hoe laat wordt het donker?
*hoo laht wordt het **don**-ker*

■ **MAPS, GUIDES...** ■ **SIGHTSEEING & TOURIST OFFICE**

ZONNIG	CLEAR / SUNNY
REGEN	RAIN
MIST	FOG
BEWOLKT	CLOUDY

It's sunny
De zon schijnt
du zon scheint

It's raining
Het regent
het ray-CHent

It's snowing
Het sneeuwt
het snaywt

It's windy
Het waait
het waheet

What a lovely day!
Wat een mooie dag!
wat un mohee-yu daCH

What awful weather!
Wat een verschrikkelijk weer!
wat un ver-schrik-ku-luk wayr

What will the weather be like tomorrow?
Wat voor weer krijgen we morgen?
wat vohr wayr krei-CHu wu mor-CHu

Do you think it will rain?
Gaat het regenen?
CHaht het ray-CHu-nu

Do I need an umbrella?
Heb ik een paraplu nodig?
heb ik un pah-rah-pluu noh-diCH

When will it stop raining?
Wanneer stopt het met regenen?
wan-nayr stopt het met ray-CHu-nu

It's very hot
Het is erg heet
het is erCH hayt

Do you think there will be a storm?
Komt er storm?
komt er storm

Do you think it will snow?
Gaat het sneeuwen?
CHaht het snay-wu

What is the temperature?
Wat is de temperatuur?
wat is du tem-pu-rah-tuur

Is the ice strong enough for skating?
Is het ijs sterk genoeg om te schaatsen?
is het eis sterk CHu-nooCH om tu schaht-su

■ MAKING FRIENDS

What work do you do?
Wat voor werk doet u?
wat vohr werk doot uu

Do you enjoy it?
Vindt u het leuk?
vindt uu het leuk

I'm... **a doctor**
Ik ben... dokter
ik ben... dok-tur

a teacher (male/female)
leraar / lerares
le-rahr / le-rah-res

I work in... **a shop**
Ik werk in... een winkel
ik werk in... un win-kel

a factory **a bank**
een fabriek een bank
un fah-breek un bank

I work from home
Ik werk thuis
ik werk tuis

I'm self-employed
Ik ben zelfstandig ondernemer
ik ben zelf-stan-diCH on-der-nay-mer

I have been unemployed for...
Ik ben ... werkloos
ik ben ... werk-lohs

...months
...maanden
...mahn-du

It's very difficult at the moment to get a job
Het is op dit moment erg moeilijk een baan te vinden
het is op dit moh-ment erCH mooee-luk un bahn tu vin-du

What are your hours?
Wat zijn uw werktijden?
wat zein uuw werk-tei-du

I work from 9 to 5
Ik werk van 9 tot 5
ik werk van nay-CHu tot veif

from Monday to Friday
van maandag tot en met vrijdag
van mahn-daCH tot en met vrei-daCH

How much holiday do you get?
Hoeveel vakantie krijgt u?
hoo-vayl vah-kan-tsee kreiCHt uu

What do you want to be when you grow up?
Wat wil je worden als je groter bent?
wat wil yu wor-du als yu CHroh-tur bent

■ MAKING FRIENDS ■ OFFICE

NOUNS AND ARTICLES

Unlike English, Dutch nouns have a gender: they are either *common* (with the article **de**) or *neuter* (with the article **het**). Therefore the words for **the** must agree with the noun they accompany – whether *common*, *neuter* or *plural*:

		pronunciation
the garden	de tuin	*du tuin*
the house	het huis	*het huis*
the garden	de tuinen	*du **tui**-nu*
the houses	de huizen	*du **hui**-zu*

NOTE:

a garden	een tuin	*un tuin*
a house	een huis	*un huis*

The Dutch word **een** can have two meanings: **a** or **one**, with a different pronunciation denoting the meaning:

a	een	*un*
one	een /**één**	*ayn*

The Dutch frequently use diminutives, expressing smallness of size, endearment or contempt. The diminutive is mostly formed by adding -**je** or -**tje**, but also -**etje**, -**pje** and -**kje**:

house	het huisje	*het **huis**-yu*
garden	het tuintje	*het **tuin**-chu*
flag	het vlaggetje	*het **vlaCH**-CHu-chu*
tree	het boompje	*het **bohm**-p-yu*
king	het koninkje	*het **koh**-nink-yu*

Diminutives are always *neuter* nouns.

PLURAL

There are three ways to form the plural of nouns. The usual way is by adding -**en**:

	singular		plural
tent	**tent** *tent*		**tenten** *ten-tu*

NOTE:

1. Nouns ending with double vowels followed by a consonant drop a vowel in the plural:

moon	**maan** *mahn*	manen **mah**-nu
leg	**been** *bayn*	benen **bay**-nu
school	**school** *schohl*	scholenn **schoh**-lu
wall	**muur** *muur*	muren **muu**-ru

2. Many nouns ending with a single vowel followed by a consonant double that consonant in the plural:

man	**man** *man*	mannen **man**-nu
bell	**bel** *bel*	bellen **bel**-lu
bone	**bot** *bot*	botten **bot**-tu

but:

day	**dag** *daCH*	dagen **dah**-CHu
town	**stad** *stad*	steden **stay**-du

3. Many nouns ending with **-s** or **-f** get **-z** and **-v** in the plural:

house	**huis** *huis*	huizen **hui**-zu
cousin/nephew	**neef** *nayf*	neven **nay**-vu

but:

cherry	**kers** *kers*	kersen **ker**-su

4. Nouns ending with a vowel or with **-aar**, **-el**, **-em**, **-en**, **-er**, **-erd**, **-je** form the plural with **-s**; here are some examples:

car	**auto** *ou-toh*	auto's *ou-tohs*
umbrella	**paraplu** *pah-rah-pluu*	paraplu's *pah-rah-pluus*
widower	**weduwnaar** *way-duuw-nahr*	weduwnaars *way-duuw-nahrs*
wing	**vleugel** *vleu-CHel*	vleugels *vleu-CHels*
broom	**bezem** *bay-zem*	bezems *bay-zems*

5. A few nouns form the plural with **-eren**:

child	**kind** *kint*	kinderen **kin**-du-ren

DEMONSTRATIVES (this, that, these, those)

Demonstratives depend on the gender of the noun:

	this	**that**	**these**	**those**
de tuin	deze tuin	die tuin	deze tuinen	die tuinen
het huis	dit huis	dat huis	deze huizen	die huizen

NOTE: pronunciation **deze**: *day-zu*

ADJECTIVES

The adjective is placed before the noun as follows:

beautiful	**mooi** *mohee*	
	de mooie tuin	de **mohee**-yu tuin
	een mooie tuin	un **mohee**-yu tuin
	het mooie huis	het **mohee**-yu huis
	een mooi huis	un **mohee** huis

PRONOUNS

Subject pronouns:

I	ik
you	jij/je
you	u *(single and plural: polite, formal)*
he	hij
she	zij/ze
it	hot
we	wij/we
you	jullie
they	zij/ze

Object pronouns:

me	me
you	je
you	u *(single and plural: polite, formal)*
him	hem
her	haar
it	het
we	ons

| you | jullie |
| they | hen |

Possessive pronouns:

mine	mijn
yours	jouw
yours	uw *(single and plural: polite, formal)*
his	zijn
hers	haar
its	–
ours	onze/ons
yours	jullie
their	hun

NOTE: | <u>de</u> tuin | <u>onze</u> tuin |
| <u>het</u> huis | <u>ons</u> huis |

QUESTIONS

who/whom	wie
what	wat
why	waarom
which	welke/welk

NOTE: | <u>de</u> tuin | <u>welke</u> tuine |
| <u>het</u> huis | <u>welk</u> huis |

VERBS

Some useful verbs:

	present	past
<u>to be</u> zijn		
I	ben	was
you	bent	was
he/she/it	is	was
we	zijn	waren
you	zijn	waren
they	zijn	waren

	present	past
to have hebben		
I	heb	had
you	hebt	had
he/she/it	heeft	had
we	hebben	hadden
you	hebben	hadden
they	hebben	hadden

	present	past
to be allowed mogen		
I	mag	mocht
you	mag	mocht
he/she/it	mag	mocht
we	mogen	mochten
you	mogen	mochten
they	mogen	mochten

	present	past
to have to moeten		
I	moet	moest
you	moet	moest
he/she/it	moet	moest
we	moeten	moesten
you	moeten	moesten
they	moeten	moesten

	present	past
to want to willen		
I	wil	wou, wilde
you	wilt	wou, wilde
he/she/it	wil	wou, wilde
we	willen	wilden
you	willen	wilden
they	willen	wilden

NOTE: When **jij** follows the verb, the end **-t** of the verb is lost:

you have	**jij hebt**
have you?	**heb jij?**

you want	**jij wilt**
do you want?	**wil jij?**

The English continuous form is unknown in Dutch:

I am going away	**ik ga weg**
I am going home	**ik ga naar huis**

equally:

are you going home?	**ga jij naar huis?**
do you go home?	**ga jij naar huis?**
do not go!	**ga niet!**

DICTIONARY
ENGLISH-DUTCH
DUTCH-ENGLISH

a	een
abbey	abdij, de
about (*relating to*)	over
(*approximately*)	in
above	boven
above the house	*boven het huis*
accident	ongeluk, het
accommodation	onderdak, het
ache *n*	pijn, de
adaptor (*electrical*)	transformator, de
address	adres, het
adhesive tape	plakband, het
admission charge	toegangsprijs, de
adult	volwassene, de
advance: *in advance*	*vooruit*
advertisement	advertentie, de
advice	advies, het
advise	adviseren
can you advise me?	*kunt u mij adviseren?*
after	na
afternoon	middag, de
again	weer
against	tegen
age	leeftijd, de
agency	agentschap, het
agent	agent, de
ago	geleden
a week ago	*een week geleden*
air-conditioning	airconditioning, de
airline	luchtvaartmaatschappij, de
air mail	luchtpost, de
air-mattress	luchtmatras, de
airport	vliegveld, het
aisle	gangpad, het

alarm	alarm, het
alarm clock	wekker, de
alcohol	alcohol, de
alcoholic	alcoholisch
is it alcoholic?	*is het alcoholisch?*
all	al ; alle ; alles
allergic to	allergisch voor
allow	toestaan
all right *(agreed)*	goed ; o.k.
are you all right?	*bent u o.k?*
almond	amandel, de
almost	bijna
alone	alleen
also	ook
always	altijd
am	see **(to be) GRAMMAR**
ambulance	ambulance, de
America	Amerika
American *(person)*	Amerikaan
American	Amerikaans
anaesthetic n	verdoving, de
and	en
angry	boos
another	nog een
answer n	antwoord, het
answer vb	antwoorden
antibiotic n	antibioticum, het
antifreeze	antivriesmiddel, het
antiseptic n	antisepticum, het
any	enig ; ieder ; een
have you any pears?	*heeft u peren?*
apartment	appartement, het
appendicitis	blindedarmontsteking, de
apple	appel, de

appointment	afspraak, de
approximately	ongeveer
apricot	abrikoos, de
are	*see* **(to be) GRAMMAR**
arm	arm, de
armbands *(swimming)*	zwemband, de
armchair	leunstoel, de
arrange	regelen
arrest vb	arresteren
arrival	aankomst, de
arrive	aankomen
art gallery	gallerie, de
arthritis	reumatiek, de
artichoke	artisjok, de
ashtray	asbak, de
ask *(for something)*	vragen
may I ask a favour?	*mag ik u een dienst vragen?*
asparagus	asperge, de
aspirin	aspirine, de
asthma	astma, de
at	bij
at home	*thuis*
attractive *(person)*	aantrekkelijk
aubergine	aubergine, de
auction	openbare verkoop, de
aunt	tante, de
Australia	Australië
Australian *(person)*	Autraliër
Australian	Australisch
automatic	automatisch
autumn	herfst, de
avocado	avocado, de
avoid	vermijden
awful	verschrikkelijk

baby	baby, de
baby food	babyvoeding, de
babysitter	oppas, de
bachelor	vrijgezel, de
back *(of body)*	rug, de
backpack	rugzak, de
bacon	bacon, het ; spek, het
bad *(weather, news)*	slecht
(fruit and vegetables)	bedorven
bag	tas, de
(suitcase)	koffer, de
(handbag)	handtas, de
baggage	bagage, de
baggage reclaim *(sign)*	bagage
baker's	bakker, de
balcony	balkon, het
bald *(person)*	kaal
(tyre)	versleten
ball	bal, de
banana	banaan, de
band *(musical)*	band, de
bandage	verband, het
bank	bank, de
bar	bar, de
barber's	kapper, de
bark vb *(dog)*	blaffen
basket	mand, de
bath	bad, het
to have a bath	in bad gaan
bathing cap	badmuts, de
bathroom	badkamer, de
battery	batterij, de
(in car)	accu, de
be	see **(to be)** GRAMMAR

beach	strand, het
bean	boon, de
(kidney bean)	witte boon, de
beautiful	mooi
bed	bed, het
bedding	beddegoed, het
bedroom	slaapkamer, de
beef	rundvlees, het
beer	bier, het
beetroot	rode biet, de
before	voor
beggar	bedelaar, de
begin	beginnen
behind	achter
behind the house	achter het huis
believe	geloven
bell	klok, de
(electric)	bel, de
below	onder
belt	riem, de
beside	naast
best	beste
better	beter
between	tussen
bicycle	fiets, de
by bicycle	met de fiots
big	groot
bigger	groter
bikini	bikini, de
bill	rekening, de
bin	vuilnisbak, de
bin liner	vuilniszak, de
binoculars	verrekijker, de
bird	vogel, de

birth	geboorte, de
birthday	verjaardag, de
birthday card	verjaardagskaart, de
birthday party	verjaardagsfeest, het
biscuit	biscuitje, het ; koekje, het
bit	stuk, het
a bit	*een beetje*
bite *vb*	bijten
bite *n*	beet, de
(insect)	insectenbeet, de
bitter	bitter
black	zwart
blackcurrant	zwartebes, de
blade *(shaving)*	mesje, het
blanket	deken, de
bleach	bleekmiddel, het
blind *(person)*	blind
(on window)	luik, het
blister	blaar, de
blocked *(road, pipe)*	geblokkeerd ; verstopt
blood	bloed, het
blood group	bloedgroep, de
blouse	blouse, de
blow-dry	drogen
blue	blauw
(light blue)	lichtblauw
boarding card	instapkaart, de
boarding house	pension, het
boat	boot, de
boat trip	boottocht, de
boil	koken
boiled egg	*gekookt ei*
bone	been, het
book *n*	boek, het

book *vb*	boeken ; reserveren
booking	reservering, de
booking office *(sign)*	reserveringen
bookshop	boekwinkel, de
boot	laars, de
(of car)	bagageruimte, de
border	grens, de
boring	saai
boss	baas, de
both	allebei
bottle	fles, de
bottle bank	glascontainer, de
bottle opener	flessenopener, de
box	doos, de
box office *(sign)*	kaartverkoop
boy	jongen, de
boyfriend	vriend, de
bra	beha, de
bracelet	armband, de
brake	rem, de
brake fluid	remvloeistof, de
brand *(of cigarettes, etc.)*	merk, het
brandy	cognac, de
bread	brood, het
break *vb*	breken
breakable	breekbaar
breakdown *(car)*	autopech, het
(nervous)	zenuwinstorting, de
breakdown van	reparatiewagen, de
breakfast	ontbijt, het
breast *(chicken)*	borst, de
breathe	ademhalen
briefcase	aktentas, de

bridge	brug, de
(game)	bridge
bring	brengen
Britain	Groot-Brittannië
British	Brits
brochure	brochure, de ; folder, de
broken	gebroken
broken down *(machine, etc.)*	kapot
brooch	broche, de
broom	bezem, de
brother	broer, de
brown	bruin
browse	rondkijken
I'm just browsing	*ik kijk alleen*
brush	borstel, de
Brussels sprouts	spruiten, de
bucket	emmer, de
buffet	restauratie, de
buffet car	restauratiewagen, de
building	gebouw, het
bulb *(flower)*	(bloem) bol, de
(electric)	gloeilamp, de
bulb field	(bloem) bollenveld, het
bull	stier, de
bun *(bread roll)*	broodje, het
bureau de change	wisselkantoor, het
burst: *a burst tyre*	*een lekke band*
bus	bus, de
business *(company)*	bedrijf, het
(general)	zaken, de
bus station	busstation, het
bus stop	bushalte, de
bus ticket	buskaartje, het
bus tour	bustocht, de

busy	druk
but	maar
butcher's	slager, de
butter	boter, de
butterfly	vlinder, de
button	knoop, de
buy	kopen
by *(via)*	via
(beside)	naast
bypass	omleiding, de
cabaret	cabaret, het
cabbage	kool, de
café *(bar)*	café, het
(coffeeshop)	coffeeshop, de
cake	cake, de ; taart, de
calculator	rekenmachine, de
call *n (telephone)*	telefoongesprek, het
a long distance call	*interlokaal telefoongesprek*
call *vb (shout)*	roepen
(by phone)	opbellen
calm	kalm
camcorder	camcorder, de
camera	camera, de
camp	kamp, het
camper *(car)*	kampeerauto, de
campsite	camping, de ; kampeerplaats, de
can *n*	blik, het
can *vb (be able)*	kunnen
can I ...?	*kan ik ...?*
Canada	Canada
Canadian	Canadees
canal	kanaal, het

111

cancel	annuleren
canoe	kano, de
canoeing	kanoën
can opener	blikopener, de
car	auto, de
carafe	karaf, de
caravan	caravan, de
carburettor	carburateur, de
card *(greetings, playing)*	kaart, de
cardigan	vest, het
careful	voorzichtig
be careful!	wees voorzichtig
car ferry	autoveerboot, de
car park	parkeerplaats, de
carpet	tapijt, het
(fitted)	vloerbedekking, de
carriage *(railway)*	wagen, de
carrot	peen,de ; wortel, de
carry	dragen
car wash	carwash, de
case *(suitcase)*	koffer, de
cash *n*	geld, het (contant)
cash *vb (cheque)*	inwisselen
cash desk	kassa, de
cashier *(male)*	kassier, de
(female)	kassière, de
casino	casino, het
cassette *(tape)*	geluidscassette, de
castle	kasteel, het
cat	kat, de
catch *(bus, train, etc.)*	nemen
cathedral	kathedraal, de
Catholic	katholiek
cauliflower	bloemkool, de

cause vb	veroorzaken
cave	grot, de
celery	selderie, de
cemetery	begraafplaats, de
centimetre	centimeter
centre (town)	centrum, het
century	eeuw, de
cereal (for breakfast)	cornflakes, de
certain (sure)	zeker
certificate	certificaat, het
chain	ketting, de
chair	stoel, de
champagne	champagne, de
chance	kans, de
change n	kleingeld, de
(small coins)	muntgeld, het
(money returned)	geld terug
change vb (money)	wisselen
changing room (shop)	paskamer, de
(sport)	kleedkamer, de
chapel	kapel, de
(Roman Catholic)	kerk, de
charge n (cost)	kosten, de
charge vb (money)	rekenen
cheap	goedkoop
cheaper	goedkoper
check vb	controleren
check in (at airport)	inchecken
(at hotel)	registeren
check-in desk	balie, de
cheerio!	dag!
cheers!	proost!
cheese	kaas, de
chemist's	drogist, de

cheque	cheque, de
cheque book	chequeboek, het
cheque card	chequepas, de
cherry	kers, de
chestnut	kastanje, de
chewing gum	kauwgom, de
chicken	kip, de
chickenpox	waterpokken, de
child *(boy)*	kind, het
children *(infants)*	kinderen, de
chilli	Spaanse peper, de
chips	patat, de
chocolate	chocolade, de
chocolates	chocolaatjes, de
chop *(meat)*	karbonade, de
Christmas	Kerstmis
Merry Christmas!	*Vrolijk Kerstmis!*
Christmas Eve	vooravond van Kerstmis
church	kerk, de
cider	appelwijn, de
cigar	sigaar, de
cigarette	sigaret, de
cinema	bioscoop, de
circus	circus, het
city	stad, de
clean *adj*	schoon
clean *vb*	schoonmaken
cleansing material	schoonmaakmiddel, het
client	cliënt, de ; klant, de
climbing	klimmen
cloakroom	garderobe, de
clock	klok, de
clogs	klompen, de

close adj (near)	vlakbij
is it close by?	is het vlakbij?
close vb	sluiten
closed	gesloten
cloth (rag)	doek, de
clothes	kleren, de
clothes peg	kleerhanger, de
cloudy	bewolkt
clove (garlic)	teentje, het
(spice)	kruidnagel, de
club	club, de
coach (bus)	bus, de
(train)	rijtuig, het
coach trip	bustocht, de
coast	kust, de
coastguard	kustwacht, de
coat	jas, de
coat hanger	jashanger, de
cocoa	cacao, de
coconut	kokosnoot, de
coffee	koffie, de
white coffee	koffie met melk
black coffee	zwarte koffie
coin	munt
Coke®	Coca Cola
colander	vergiet, het
cold n	verkoudheid, de
cold adj	koud
I'm cold	ik heb het koud
colour	kleur, de
comb	kam, de
come	komen
(arrive)	aankomen
come back	terugkomen

come in	binnenkomen
come in!	*kom binnen!*
comfortable	gerieflijk
communion	communie, de
company	gezelschap, het
compartment	compartiment, het ; coupé, de
complain	klagen
complaint	klacht, de
compulsory	verplicht
computer	computer, de
concert	concert, het
conditioner	conditioner, de
condom	condoom, het
conductor *(on bus)*	conducteur, de
conference	conferentie, de
confirm	bevestigen
congratulations	gelukwensen, de
connection *(train)*	aansluiting, de
constipated	verstopt
consulate	consulaat, het
contact *vb*	contact opnemen met
contact lens cleaner	contactlens-schoonmaakmiddel, het
contact lenses	contactlenzen, de
contraceptive *n*	voorbehoedsmiddel, het
cook *n*	kok, de
cook *vb*	koken
cooker	kooktoestel, het
cool	koel
copy *n*	kopie, de
copy *vb*	kopiëren
corkscrew	kurketrekker, de
corner	hoek, de
cosmetics	schoonheidsmiddelen, de

cost n	kosten
cot	kinderbedje, het
cotton	katoen, het
cotton wool	watten, de
couchette	slaapwagen, de
cough n	hoest, de
cough sweets	hoesttabletten, de
country (not town)	platteland, het
(nation)	land, het
couple (2 people)	paar, het
courgettes	courgettes, de
courier (tour guide)	geleider, de
course (of meal)	gang, de
cousin (male)	neef, de
(female)	nicht, de
cover charge	couvert, het
cow	koe, de
crab	krab, de
crash (two cars, etc.)	ongeluk, het
crash helmet	valhelm, de
cream (lotion)	crème, de
(on milk)	room, de
credit card	creditcard, de
crisps	chips, de
cross vb	kruisen
crossing (road)	kruispunt, het
crowded	druk
cruise n	cruise, de
cucumber	komkommer, de
cup	kop, de
cupboard	kast, de
currant	krent, de
current	actueel
cushion	kussen, het

custard	vla, de
customer	klant, de
customs (at border)	douane, de
customs	gewoonten, de
cut n	snee, de
cut vb	snijden
cutlery	bestek, het
cycle vb	fietsen
cycle (bike) n	fiets, de

daily (each day)	dagelijks
damage	schade, de
damp	vochtig
dance n	dans, de
dance vb	dansen
dangerous	gevaarlijk
Danish	Deens
dark	donker
date	datum, de
date of birth	geboortedatum, de
daughter	dochter, de
day	dag, de
day ticket	dagkaart, de
dead	dood
dear	lieve
(expensive)	duur
decaffeinated coffee	koffie zonder caffeïne, de
deck chair	dekstoel, de
declare	aangeven
deep	diep
deep freeze	diepvries, de
defrost	ontdooien

delay *n*	vertraging, de
delay *vb*	vertragen
delicious	heerlijk
Denmark	Denemarken
dentist	tandarts, de
dentures	kunstgebit, het
deodorant	deodorant, de
department store	warenhuis, het
departure	vertrek, het
departure lounge	vertrekhal, de
deposit *n*	deposito, de ; waarborgsom, de
dessert	nagerecht, het
details	details, de
detergent	wasmiddel, het
detour	omweg, de
develop	ontwikkelen
diabetic	(lijdend aan) suikerziekte
dialling code	netnummer, het
diamond	diamant, de
diarrhoea	diarree, de
diary	dagboek, het
dictionary	woordenboek, het
diesel	diesel
diet	dieet, het
different	verschillend
difficult	moeilijk
dinghy	jol, de
(rubber)	rubberboot, de
dining room	eetkamer, de
dinner	diner, het
to have dinner	dineren
direct *(train, etc.)*	rechtstreeks
directory	adresboek, het
directory *(telephone)*	telefoonboek, het

dirty	vuil
disabled	invalide
disco	disco, de
dish	bord, het
dishtowel	theedoek, de
dishwasher	afwasmachine, de
disinfectant	ontsmettingsmiddel, het
distilled water	gedistilleerd water, het
dive	duiken
diver	duiker, de
divorced	gescheiden
dizzy	duizelig
do	doen
doctor	dokter, de
documents	documenten, de
dog	hond, de
doll	pop, de
dollar	dollar, de
door	deur, de
double	dubbel
double bed	tweepersoonsbed, het
double room	tweepersoonskamer, de
down *(below)*	beneden
drains *(sewage system)*	riolering, de
draught *(air)*	tocht, de
(beer)	van 't vat
dress n	jurk, de
dress vb *(get dressed)*	kleden
dressing *(for food)*	saus, de
drink n	drank, de
drink vb	drinken
drinking chocolate	chocolademelk, de
drinking water	drinkwater, het

drive	**rijden**
driver (of car)	**bestuurder, de**
driving licence	**rijbewijs, het**
drown	**verdrinken**
drug (medicinal)	**geneesmiddel, het**
drunk	**dronken**
dry adj	**droog**
dry vb	**drogen**
dry-cleaner's	**stomerij, de**
duck	**eend, de**
due: *when is it due?*	*wanneer komt het?*
dummy (for baby)	**speen, de**
during	**tijdens**
dust	**stof, het**
Dutch	**Nederlands**
Dutchman	**Nederlander, de**
Dutch woman	**Nederlandse, de**
duty-free shop	**belastingvrije winkel, de**
duvet	**dekbed, het**
dynamo	**dynamo, de**

each	**ieder**
ear	**oor, het**
earache	**oorpijn, de**
I have earache	*ik heb oorpijn*
earlier	**vroeger**
early	**vroeg**
earn	**verdienen**
earrings	**oorbellen, de**
earth	**aarde, de**
earthquake	**aardbeving, de**
east	**oost**

Easter	Pasen
easy	gemakkelijk
eat	eten
eel	aal, de ; paling, de
egg	ei, het
eggs	eieren, de
fried egg	*gebakken ei*
hard-boiled egg	*hardgekookt ei*
scrambled eggs	*roereieren*
either	beide
either one	*allebei*
elastic	elastiek, het
electric	elektrisch
electrician	elektricien, de
electricity	elektriciteit, de
electricity meter	elektriciteitsmeter, de
embassy	ambassade, de
emergency	noodgeval, het
empty	leeg
end	einde, het
engaged *(to be married)*	verloofd
(toilet)	bezet
engine	motor, de
engineer *(car)*	mechanicien, de
England	Engeland
English	Engels
enjoy	genieten
enjoy your meal!	*eet smakelijk!*
I enjoy swimming	*ik hou van zwemmen*
enough	genoeg
enquiry desk	inlichtingenloket, het
enter	binnenkomen
entertainments	amusement, het
enthusiastic	enthousiast

entrance	ingang, de
entrance fee	toegangsgeld, het
envelope	envelop, de
equipment	uitrusting, de
escalator	roltrap, de
essential	essentieel
Eurocheque	Eurocheque, de
Europe	Europa
European	Europees
evening	avond, de
in the evening	*'s avonds*
evening meal	avondeten, het
every	alle ; ieder
everyone	iedereen
everything	alles
exact	precies
examination	examen, het
example	voorbeeld, het
for example	*bijvoorbeeld*
excellent	uitmuntend
except	behalve
excess luggage	overvracht, de
exchange *(tourist) n*	wisselkantoor, het
exchange *vb*	wisselen
exchange rate	wisselkoers, de
exciting	opwindend
excursion	excursie, de
excuse *vb*	verontschuldigen
excuse me!	*pardon!*
exercise book	oefenboek, het
exhibition	tentoonstelling, de
exit	uitgang, de
expect	verwachten
expert	expert, de

expire (ticket, passport)	verlopen
explain	uitleggen
express n (train)	sneltrein, de
express letter	expresspost
extra	extra
eye	oog, het
eyelash	ooglid, het
fabric	stof, de
face	gezicht, het
facilities	faciliteiten, de
factory	fabriek, de
fainted	flauwgevallen
fair (funfair)	kermis, de
(hair)	blond
fake	namaak
fall vb	vallen
he/she has fallen	hij/zij is gevallen
family (small)	gezin, het
(large)	familie, de
famous	beroemd
fan (electric)	ventilator, de
(paper)	waaier, de
(football)	supporter, de
(cinema, jazz, etc.)	fan, de
fan belt	aandrijfsnaar, de
far	ver
how far is ...?	hoe ver is ...?
fare	reiskosten, de
farm	boerderij, de
farmer	boer, de
fashionable	modieus
fast	snel

fat	vet
father	vader, de
father-in-law	schoonvader, de
fault	fout, de
it's not my fault	*het is niet mijn schuld*
favourite	favoriet
feather	veer, de
feed *vb*	voeden
feel	voelen
I don't feel well	*ik voel me niet goed*
to feel sick	*ik voel me ziek*
feminine	vrouwelijk
fence	schutting, de ; hek, het
ferry	veer, het ; pont, de
fetch *(bring)*	halen
(go and get)	brengen
fever	koorts, de
few	enkele ; weinig
a few	*enkele*
fiancé(e)	verloofde, de
field	veld, het
fight *vb*	vechten
file *(computer)*	file, het ; archief, het
(nail)	vijl, de
fill	vullen
(fill in form)	invullen
fill it up, please!	*volmaken, alstublieft!*
filling *(in tooth)*	vulling, de
film *(at cinema, for camera)*	film, de
fine *adj (weather)*	mooi
fine *n (to be paid)*	boete, de
finger	vinger, de
finish	eindigen ; afmaken
fire	brand, de
fire!	*brand!*

125

fire brigade	brandweer, de
fire extinguisher	brandblusser, de
fireworks	vuurwerk, het
first	eerste
first aid	eerste hulp *(sign:* **EHBO**)
first class	eerste klas, de
first floor	eerste verdieping, de
first name	voornaam, de
fish *n*	vis, de
fish *vb*	vissen
fishing rod	hengel, de
fit *adj (healthy)*	fit
fit *vb (clothes)*	passen
fizzy	mousserend
flag	de vlag
flask *(thermos)*	thermosfles, de
flat *(apartment)*	flat, de
(level)	plat
(battery)	leeg
flat tyre	lekke band, de
flavour	smaak, de
flea	vlooi, de
flight	vlucht, de
flood	vloed, de
floor *(of building)*	verdieping, de
(of room)	vloer, de
flour	bloem, de
flower	bloem, de
flu	griep, de
fly	vlieg, de
fly sheet	vliegenpapier, het
fog	mist, de
foggy	mistig
it's foggy	*het is mistig*

foil	folie, de
fold *vb*	vouwen
follow	volgen
food	voedsel, het
food poisoning	voedselvergiftiging, de
foot	voet, de
on foot	*te voet*
football	voetbal, het
for *(in exchange for)*	voor
for you	*voor jou*
foreign	buitenlands
forest	woud, het
forget	vergeten
forgive	vergeven
fork	de vork
(in road)	splitsing, de
form *(document)*	formulier, het
fortnight	twee weken
fountain	fontein, de
fracture	breuk, de
France	Frankrijk
free *(not occupied)*	vrij
(costing nothing)	gratis
freezer	vrieskast, de
French	Frans
french beans	snijbonen, de
frequent	vaak
fresh *(food)*	verse
fresh milk	*verse melk*
fresh orange juice	*geperste sinaasappel*
fridge	koelkast, de
fried	gebakken
friend *(man)*	vriend, de
(female)	vriendin, de

frightened	bang
fringe	franje, de
from	van, uit
front	voorkant, de
in front of the building	voor het gebouw
frozen (food)	diepvries
fruit	fruit, het
fruits	vruchten, de
fruit juice	vruchtesap, het
fruit salad	vruchtensalade, de
frying pan	koekepan, de
fuel	brandstof, de
full	vol
full board	vol pension
fumes	dampen, de
funeral	begrafenis, de
funfair	kermis, de
funny (amusing)	leuk
(strange)	raar
fur	bont
furniture	meubelen, de
fuse	zekering, de
gallery	gallerij, de
gallon	= approx. 4.5 litres
gambling	gokken
game	spel, het
garage	garage, de
garden	tuin, de
garlic	knoflook, de
gas	gas, het
gas cylinder	gashouder, de

gears	versnellingen, de
gentleman	heer, de
gents *(toilets)*	heren
genuine	echt
German	Duits
German measles	rode hond, de
Germany	Duitsland
get *(obtain)*	halen
(receive)	krijgen
(fetch)	brengen
get in *(vehicle)*	instappen
get off *(bus, metro, etc.)*	uitstappen
gift	cadeau, het
gift shop	cadeauwinkel, de
ginger	gember, de
girl	meisje, het
girlfriend	vriendin, de
give	geven
give back	teruggeven
glass *(for drinking, substance)*	glas, het
glasses	bril, de
gloves	handschoenen, de
glucose	glucose, de
glue	lijm, de
go	gaan
go back	teruggaan
go down(stairs)	naar beneden gaan
go in	binnengaan
go out	naar buiten gaan
goggles *(swimming)*	zwembril, de
gold	goud, het
golf	golf
golf course	golfbaan, de

good	goed
good afternoon	goedemiddag
goodbye	dag
good evening	goedenavond
good morning	goedemorgen
good night	goedenacht
goose	gans, de
gramme	gram, het
grandfather	grootvader, de
grandmother	grootmoeder, de
grape	druif, de
grapefruit	grapefruit, de
grass	gras, het
greasy	vet
green	groen
green card	verzekeringskaart, de
grey	grijs
grilled	gegrild
grocer's	kruidenier, de
ground	grond, de
ground floor	benedenverdieping, de
groundsheet	grondzeil, het
group	groep, de
guarantee	garantie, de
guard (on train)	controleur, de
guest	gast, de
guesthouse	pension, het
guide n	gids, de
guide vb	leiden
guidebook	reisgids, de
guided tour	rondgang met gids, de
gym shoes	gymschoenen, de

haemorrhoids	aambeien, de
hair	haar, het
hairbrush	haarborstel, de
haircut	haar knippen
hairdresser	kapper, de
hairdryer	haardroger, de
hairgrip	haarspeld, de
hair spray	hairspray, de
half	half
a half litre of ...	*een halve liter ...*
ham	ham, de
hand	hand, de
handbag	handtas, de
handicapped	gehandicapt
handkerchief	zakdoek, de
hand luggage	handbagage, de
hand-made	met de hand gemaakt
hangover	kater, de
happen	gebeuren
what happened?	*wat gebeurt er?*
happy	gelukkig
harbour	haven, de
hard	hard
hat	hoed, de
have	hebben
hay fever	hooikoorts, de
hazelnut	hazelnoot, de
he	hij
head	hoofd, het
headache	hoofdpijn, de
I have a headache	*ik heb hoofdpijn*
head waiter	oberkelner, de
hear	horen
heart	hart, het

heart attack	hartaanval, de
heater	kachel, de
heating	verwarming, de
heavy	zwaar
hello	hallo
help n	hulp, de
help!	*help!*
help vb	helpen
can you help me?	*kunt u mij helpen?*
herb	kruid, het
here	hier
high	hoog
high blood pressure	hoge bloeddruk
high chair	kinderstoel, de
high tide	vloed, de
hill	heuvel, de
hire	huren
hit	raken
hitchhike	liften
hold	houden
(contain)	bevatten
hold-up *(traffic jam)*	vertraging, de
hole	gat, het
holiday	vakantie, de
(public)	vrije dag, de ; feestdag, de
on holiday	*op vakantie*
Holland	Holland
home	huis, het
at home	*thuis*
honey	honing, de
honeymoon	huwelijksreis, de
hope	hopen
I hope so/not	*ik hoop het/niet*
hors d'œuvre	voorgerecht, het

horse	paard, het
hose	slang, de
hospital	ziekenhuis, het
hot	heet
I'm hot	ik heb het heet/warm
it's hot (weather)	het is heet
hotel	hotel, het
hour	uur, het
house	huis, het
house wine	huiswijn, de
hovercraft	hovercraft, de
how (in what way)	hoe
how much/many?	hoeveel?
how are you?	hoe gaat het?
hungry	hongerig
I'm hungry	ik heb honger
hurry	haast, de
I'm in a hurry	ik heb haast
hurt (cause pain)	pijn doen
my back hurts	mijn rug doet pijn
husband	echtgenoot, de
hydrofoil	vleugelboot, de
I	ik
ice	ijs, het
ice cream	ijs, het
iced (drink)	met ijs
ice lolly	ijslolly, de
ice rink	ijsbaan, de
if	als ; wanneer ; indien
ignition	ontsteking, de
ignition key (car)	autosleutel, de

ill	ziek
immediately	onmiddellijk
important	belangrijk
impossible	onmogelijk
in	in ; over
in 10 minutes	over 10 minuten
inch	= approx. 2.5 cm
included	inclusief
indigestion	indigestie, de
indoors	binnen
(at home)	thuis ; in huis
infectious	besmettelijk
information	informatie, de
information office	informatiekantoor, het
injection	inenting, de
injury	wond, de ; blessure, de
injured	gewond ; geblesseerd
ink	inkt, de
insect	insect, het
insect bite	insectenbeet, de
insect repellent	insectenbestrijdingsmiddel, het
inside	in ; binnen
inside the car	in de auto
instant coffee	poederkoffie, de
instead of	in plaats van
instructor	instructeur, de
insulin	insuline, de
insurance	verzekering, de
insurance certificate	verzekeringsbewijs, het
insure	verzekeren
interesting	interessant
international	internationaal
interpreter	vertaler, de
interval (theatre, etc.)	pauze, de

interview	interview, het
into	in ; naar binnen
introduce	introduceren
invitation	uitnodiging, de
invite	uitnodigen
invoice	rekening, de ; factuur, de
Ireland	Ierland
Irish	Iers
iron n (for clothes)	strijkijzer, het
(metal)	ijzer, het
iron vb	strijken
ironmonger's	ijzerwarenhandel, de
is	is see **(to be) GRAMMAR**
island	eiland, het
it	het see **GRAMMAR**
Italian	Italiaans
Italy	Italië
itch	jeuk, de
item	onderdeel, het
itemized bill	gedetailleerde rekening, de
ivory	ivoor, het
jack (for car)	krik, de
jacket	jasje, het
jam (food)	jam, de
jammed	bekneld
Japan	Japan
Japanese	Japans
jar (container)	pot, de
jaundice	geelzucht, de
jazz	jazz, de
jealous	jaloers

jeans	jeans, de ; spijkerbroek, de
jelly *(dessert)*	gelatine-pudding, de
jellyfish	kwal, de
jersey	trui, de
(football)	shirt, het
jeweller's	juwelier, de
jewellery	juwelen, de
Jewish	joods
job	baan, de
jog *vb*	hardlopen
joint *(bone)*	gewricht, het
joke	grap, de
journalist	journalist, de
journey	reis, de
judge *vb*	beoordelen
jug	kruik, de
juice	sap, het
jump	springen
jump leads	startkabel, de
junction *(road)*	afslag, de ; kruising, de
June	juni
just	net
just two	*alleen twee*
I've just arrived	*ik ben net aangekomen*

keep	houden
keep the change	*laat zo maar zitten*
kennel	kennel, de
kettle	fluitketel, de ; ketel, de
key	sleutel, de
keyboard	toetsenbord, het
key in *vb*	intypen
key-ring	sleutelhanger, de

kick	schoppen
kid (young goat)	geitje, het
kidneys	nieren, de
kill	doden
kilo	kilo, de
kilometre	kilometer, de
kind n (sort, type)	soort, het ; type, het
kind adj (person)	aardig
king	koning, de
kiosk	kiosk, de
kiss n	zoen, de ; kus, de
kiss vb	zoenen ; kussen
kitchen	keuken, de
kitten	katje, het
knee	knie, de
knickers	onderbroek, de
knife	mes, het
knit	breien
knock vb (on door)	kloppen
knock down (car)	omverrijden
knot	knoop, de
know (facts)	weten
(be acquainted with)	kennen
knowledge	kennis, de
label n	etiket, het
laces (of shoe)	schoenveters, de
ladder	ladder, de
ladies (toilet)	dames
lady	dame, de
lager	bier, het
lake	meer, het

lamb	lam, het
lamp	lamp, de
land n	land, het
land vb	landen
when does the plane land?	*wanneer landt het vliegtuig?*
lane	laan, de
(of motorway)	rijstrook, de
language	taal, de
large	groot
last	vorig
last week	*vorige week*
late	laat
the train is late	*de trein is laat*
sorry I'm late	*het spijt me dat ik te laat ben*
later	later
launderette	wasserij, de
lavatory *(in house)*	toilet, de ; w.c., het
(in public place)	toilet, de
lawyer	advocaat, de
laxative	laxeermiddel, het
layby	vluchtstrook, de
lazy	lui
lead *(electric)*	draad, de
leader	leider, de
(guide)	gids, de
leaf	blad, het
leak *(of gas, liquid, in roof)*	lek, het
learn	leren
least	minst
at least	*tenminste*
leather	leer, het
leave *(leave behind)*	achterlaten
(depart)	vertrekken
when does ... leave?	*wanneer vertrekt...?*

left	links
on/to the left	aan de linkerkant
turn left	ga linksaf
left-luggage *(office)*	bagage-depot, het
leg	been, het
legend	legende, de
lemon	citroen, de
lemonade	limonade, de
lemon tea	citroenthee, de
lend	lenen
length	lengte, de
lens *(photographic)*	lens, de
less	minder
let *(allow)*	toelaten
(hire out)	verhuren
letter	brief, de
(of alphabet)	letter, de
letterbox	brievenbus, de
lettuce	sla, de
level crossing	overweg, de
library	bibliotheek, de
licence	vergunning, de
lid	deksel, het
lie *(untruth)*	liegen
lie down	liggen
life	leven, het
lifeboat	reddingsboot, de
lifeguard	lijfwacht, de
life jacket	reddingsvest, het
lift	lift, de
lift *vb (weight)*	optillen
light *n*	vuurtje, het
have you a light?	heeft u een vuurtje?
light *vb*	aansteken

light bulb	gloeilamp, de
lighter	aansteker, de
lightning	onweer, het
like *prep*	als ; zoals
like you	zoals jij
like this	zoals dit
like *vb*	houden van
I like coffee	ik hou van koffie
lime *(fruit)*	limoen, de
line *(row, queue)*	rij, de
(telephone)	lijn, de
lip salve	lippenzalf, de
lipstick	lippenstift, de
liqueur	likeur, de
list *n*	lijst, de
listen (to)	luisteren
litre	liter, de
litter	vuilnis, het
little *(few)*	weinig
little *(small)*	klein
a little milk	een beetje melk
live	wonen
I live in Edinburgh	ik woon in Edinburg
liver	lever, de
living room	woonkamer, de
loaf	brood, het
lobster	kreeft, de
local *(wine, speciality)*	lokale
lock *vb (door)*	op slot doen
lock *n (on door, box)*	slot, het
locker *(luggage)*	kast, de
London	Londen
long	lang
for a long time	lange tijd

look at	kijken naar
look after	zorgen voor
look for	zoeken
lorry	vrachtauto, de
lose	verliezen
lost (object)	verloren
I've lost my wallet	*ik heb mijn portefeuille verloren*
I'm lost	*ik ben verdwaald*
lost property office (sign)	gevonden voorwerpen
lot (many)	veel
lotion	lotion, de
loud	luid
(volume)	hard
lounge (in hotel)	conversatiezaal, de
love n	liefde, de
love vb (person)	houden van
I love swimming	*ik hou van zwemmen*
lovely	lief
low	laag
low tide	eb, de
lucky	gelukkig
to be lucky	*geluk hebben*
luggage	bagage, de
luggage rack	bagagerek, het
luggage tag	bagagelabel, de
luggage trolley	bagagewagentje, het
lunch	lunch, de ; middageten, het
luxury	luxe, de
macaroni	macaroni, de
machine	machine, de
mackerel	makreel, de
mad	gek

magazine	tijdschrift, het
maid *(in hotel)*	kamermeisje, het
maiden name	meisjesnaam, de
main	belangrijkste
main course	hoofdgerecht, het
make n *(brand)*	merk, het
make vb *(generally)*	maken
(meal)	koken
make-up	make-up, de
male	mannelijk
man	man, de
manager	manager, de
managing director	directeur, de
manufacture vb	fabriceren
many	veel
map *(of region)*	kaart, de
(of town)	plattegrond, de
marble	marmer, het
margarine	margarine, de
mark *(stain)*	vlek, de
market	markt, de
marmalade	marmelade, de
married	getrouwd
marry *(get married to)*	trouwen
marzipan	marsepein, het
mass *(in church)*	mis, de
mast	mast, de
match *(game)*	wedstrijd, de
matches	lucifers, de
material *(cloth)*	stof, de
matter *(substance)*	materiaal, het
it doesn't matter	*het geeft niet*
what's the matter?	*wat is er aan de hand?*
mattress	het matras

mayonnaise	mayonaise, de
meadow	wei, de
meal	maaltijd, de
mean *(signify)*	betekenen
what does this mean?	wat betekent dit?
means	middelen, de
measles	mazelen, de
measure *vb*	meten
meat	vlees, het
mechanic	mechanisch
medicine	medicijn, het
medium	midden ; medium
medium rare *(meat)*	licht gebakken
meet	tegenkomen ; ontmoeten
meeting	ontmoeting, de
meeting *(to discuss)*	vergadering, de
melon	meloen, de
member *(of club, etc.)*	lid, het
men	mannen, de
menu	menu, het
meringue	schuimgebak, het
message	boodschap, de
metal	metalen, de
meter	meter, de
metre	meter
midday	twaalf uur
midnight	middernacht
migraine	migraine, de
mile	5 miles = approx. 8 km
milk	melk, de
milkshake	milkshake, de
millimetre	millimeter
million	miljoen

mince	gehakt, het
mind: do you mind?	vind je het erg?
mineral water	mineraalwater, het
minimum	minimum, het
minister (church)	dominee, de
minor road	B-weg, de
mint (herb)	munt, de
(sweet)	pepermuntje, het
minute	minuut, de
mirror	spiegel, de
miss (train, etc.)	missen
Miss	mejuffrouw
missing (thing)	vermist
my son is missing	mijn zoon wordt vermist
mistake	fout, de
misty	mistig
it's misty	het mist
misunderstanding	misverstand, het
there's been a misunderstanding	er is een misverstand
mix vb	mengen
mixture	mengsel, het
modern	modern
moisturizer	vochthoudende crème, de
monastery	klooster, het
money	geld, het
monkey	aap, de
month	maand, de
monument	monument, het
moon	maan, de
mop n (for floor)	zwabber, de
more	meer
more wine, please	nog wat wijn, alstublieft

morning	morgen, de
mosquito	muskiet, de
most	meest
most of	*de meeste van*
moth	nachtvlinder, de
(clothes)	mot, de
mother	moeder, de
mother-in-law	schoonmoeder, de
motor	motor, de
motor boat	motorboot, de
motor cycle	motorfiets, de
motorway	autoweg, de
mountain	berg, de
mouse	muis, de
moustache	snor, de
mouth	mond, de
move	bewegen
it isn't moving	*het beweegt niet*
Mr	de heer (dhr.)
Mrs	mevrouw (mevr.)
much	veel
it costs too much	*het is te duur*
mud	modder, de
mum	ma
mumps	bof, de
muscle	spier, de
museum	museum, het
mushroom	champignon, de
music	muziek, de
musician	musicus, de
mussel	mossel, de
mustard	mosterd, de
mutton	schapevlees, het
my	mijn

nail *(fingernail)*	nagel, de
(metal)	spijker, de
naked	naakt
name	naam, de
napkin	servet, het
nappy	luier, de
narrow	nauw
nationality	nationaliteit, de
navy blue	marine blauw
near	bij
near *(close)*	vlakbij
necessary	nodig
neck	nek, de
necklace	halssnoer, het
need	nodig hebben
I need an aspirin	*ik heb een aspirine nodig*
needle	naald, de
needle and thread	*naald en draad*
negative *(photography)*	negatief, het
neighbour	buur, de
nephew	neef, de
nervous	nerveus
nest	nest, het
Netherlands, the	Nederland
never	nooit
I never drink alcohol	*ik drink nooit alcohol*
new	nieuw
news	nieuws, het
newspaper	krant, de
New Year	Nieuwjaar
New Zealand	Nieuw-Zeeland
next	volgend
the next stop	*de volgende halte*
next week	*volgende week*

nice *(person)*	aardig
(place, holiday)	leuk
niece	nicht, de
night	nacht, de
night club	nachtclub, de
nightdress	nachtjapon, de
no	nee
nobody	niemand
noise	lawaai, het
non-alcoholic	zonder alcohol
none	geen
non-smoking *(sign)*	niet roken
north	noord
Northern Ireland	Noord-Ierland
nose	neus, de
not	niet
not any	geen
I don't know any	*ik ken geen*
I don't know	*ik weet het niet*
note *(bank note)*	briefje, het
(letter)	brief, de
note pad	blocnote, de
nothing	niets
nothing else	*anders niets*
notice *(sign)*	aankondiging, de
novel	roman, de
November	november
now	nu
number	nummer, het
number plate *(on car)*	nummerbord, het
nurse *(female)*	verpleegster, de
(male)	verpleger, de
nursery school	kleuterschool, de
nut *(to eat)*	noot, de
(for bolt)	moer, de

oak	eik, de
oar	roeiriem, de
oats	haver, de
obvious	duidelijk
occasionally	nu en dan
octopus	inktvis, de
odd	oneven ; gek
of	van
off (machine, etc.)	uit
this milk is off	de melk is bedorven
offence (crime)	overtreding, de
offer	aanbod, het
office	kantoor, het
often	vaak
oil	olie, de
oil filter	oliefilter, het
ointment	zalf, de
OK (agreed)	o.k.
old	oud
how old are you?	hoe oud bent u?
olive oil	olijfolie, de
olives	olijven, de
omelette	omelet, de
on (light, TV)	aan
(tap)	open
on the table	op de tafel
once	eens
at once	direct
one	één
one-way (street)	éénrichtingsverkeer
onion	ui, de
only (child)	enig
only	slechts
it costs only...	het kost slechts...

open *adj*	open
open *vb*	openen
opera	opera, de
operator *(phone, female)*	telefoniste, de
opinion	mening, de
in my opinion	volgens mij
opposite	tegenover
or	of
orange *adj*	oranje
orange *n*	sinaasappel, de
orange juice *(fresh)*	sinaasappelsap, het
orchard	boomgaard, de
order *(in pub) n*	bestelling, de
order *vb*	bestellen
organize	organiseren
other	ander
the other one	de andere
have you any others?	heeft u anderen?
ounce	= approx. 30 g
out *(light)*	uit
he's out	hij is weg
outside	buiten
outskirts	buitenwijken, de
oven	oven, de
over *(on top of)*	boven ; op
overcharge *(bill)*	te veel in rekening brengen
overcoat	overjas, de
overnight *(travel)*	gedurende de nacht
owe	verschuldigd zijn
I owe you ...	ik ben u ... verschuldigd
owner	eigenaar, de
oxygen	zuurstof, de
oyster	oester, de

pack n *(luggage)*	pak, het
pack vb	pakken
package tour	geheel verzorgde reis
packed lunch	lunchpakket, het
packet	pakje, het
padlock	hangslot, het
page	bladzijde, de
paid	betaald
painful	pijnlijk
painkiller	pijnstiller, de
painting	schilderij, het
pair	paar, het
palace	paleis, het
pale	bleek
pan	pan, de
pancake	pannekoek, de
panties	damesonderbroek, de
pants *(underwear)*	onderbroek, de
paper	papier, het
paraffin	paraffine, de
parcel	pakje, het
pardon?	pardon?
parents	ouders, de
park n	park, het
park vb	parkeren
parking disk	parkeerschijf, de
parsley	peterselie, de
part	deel, het
party *(group)*	groep, de
(celebration)	feest, het
passenger	passagier, de
passport	paspoort, het
passport control	paspoortcontrole, de

pasta	pasta, de
pastry (pie)	pastei, de
(cake)	gebak, het
pâté	paté, de
path	pad, het
pavement	stoep, de
pay vb	betalen
payment	betaling, de
peach	perzik, de
peanut	olienoot, de ; pinda, de
pear	peer, de
peas	doperwten, de
pebble	kiezel, de
pedestrian	voetganger, de
peel vb (fruit)	schillen
peg (for clothes)	knijper, de
(for tent)	haring, de
pen	pen, de
pencil	potlood, het
penicillin	penicilline, de
penknife	zakmes, het
pensioner	gepensioneerde, de
pepper (spice)	peper, de
(vegetable)	paprika, de
per	por
per hour	per uur
per week	per week
perfect	perfect
performance	prestatie, de
(musical)	voorstelling, de
perfume	parfum, het
period (menstruation)	menstruatie, de
perm	permanent, het
permit n	vergunning, de

person	persoon, de
petrol	benzine, de
petrol station	benzinestation, het
phone	see **telephone**
photocopy n	fotokopie, de
photocopy vb	fotokopiëren
photograph n	foto, de
photograph vb	fotograferen
picnic	picknick, de
picture (painting)	schilderij, het
(photo)	foto, de
pie (fruit)	vruchtentaart, de ; vlaai, de
(meat)	pastei, de
(pastry)	taart, de
piece	stuk, het
pill	pil, de
pillow	kussen, het
pillowcase	kussensloop, de
pin	speld, de
pineapple	ananas, de
pink	rose
pint	= approx. 0.5 litrer
pipe (smoker's)	pijp, de
plaster (sticking plaster)	pleister, de
plastic	plastic
plate	bord, het
platform (train)	spoor, het ; perron, het
play (games)	spel, het
playroom	speelkamer, de
please	alstublieft
pleased	tevreden
pliers	buigtang, de
plug (electrical)	stekker, de
(for sink)	stop, de

plum	pruim, de
plumber	loodgieter, de
points (in car)	bougie, de
poisonous	giftig
police	politie, de
police!	politie!
policeman	agent, de ; politie-agent, de
police station	politiebureau, het
polish (for shoes)	schoenpoetsmiddel, het
polluted	vervuild
pool (swimming)	zwembad, het
pork	varkensvlees, het
port (seaport)	haven, de
(wine)	port, de
porter	portier, de
portrait	portret, het
Portugal	Portugal
Portuguese	Portugees
possible	mogelijk
post vb	posten
postbox	brievenbus, de
PO Box	postbus, de
postcard	briefkaart, de
postcode	postcode, de
post office	postkantoor, het
pot (for cooking)	pot, de
potato	aardappel, de
pound (weight)	= approx. 0.5 kilo
(money)	pond, hot
pour	schenken
powdered milk	poedermelk, de
prawn	garnaal, de
prefer	prefereren
pregnant	zwanger

prepare	voorbereiden
prescription	recept, het
present *(gift)*	cadeau, het
pretty	mooi
price	prijs, de
price list	prijslijst, de
priest	priester, de
prince	prins, de
princess	prinses, de
private	privé
prize	prijs, de
problem	probleem, het
producer *(TV, film)*	producent, de
programme	programma, het
prohibited	verboden
pronounce	uitspreken
how's it pronounced?	*hoe spreek je het uit?*
Protestant	protestant
prune	pruim, de
public	openbaar
public holiday	algemene feestdag, de
pudding	pudding, de
pull	trekken
pullover	pullover, de
puncture	lekke band, de
purple	paars
purse	portemonnaie, de
push	duwen
pushchair	rolstoel, de
put	zetten ; leggen ; plaatsen
pyjamas	pyjama, de

quality	kwaliteit, de
quarrel *vb*	ruzie maken
quay	kade, de
queen	koningin, de
question	vraag, de
queue *n*	rij, de
queue *vb*	in de rij staan
quick	vlug
quickly	vlug
quiet *(place)*	stil
quilt	deken, de
quite	heel ; nogal
it's quite good	*het is heel goed*
it's quite expensive	*het is nogal duur*

rabbit	konijn, het
rabies	hondsdolheid, de
race *n*	ras, het
rack *(luggage)*	bagagenet, het
racket *(tennis)*	tennisracket, het
radio	radio, de
radishes	radijsjes, de
railway	spoorweg, de
railway station	station, het
rain *n*	regen, de
raincoat	regenjas, de
raining: *it's raining*	*het regent*
raisin	rozijn, de
ramp	helling, de
rare *(unique)*	zeldzaam
(steak)	rauw
rash *(on skin)*	uitslag, de
raspberry	framboos, de

rate	koers, de
rate of exchange	wisselkoers, de
raw	rauw
razor	scheermes, het
razor blades	scheermesjes, de
read	lezen
ready	klaar
to get ready	klaarmaken
real	echt
realise	realiseren
reason	reden, de
receipt	kassabon, de
recently	recentelijk
reception (desk)	receptie, de
recipe	recept, het
recognize	herkennen
recommend	aanbevelen
record (music)	plaat, de
red	rood
redcurrant	rode bes, de
reduction	korting, de
reel	spoel, de
refill (for pen)	vulling, de
refund vb	terugbetalen
registered	geregistreerd
reimburse	vergoeden
relation (family)	relatie, de
relax	relaxen
reliable (method)	betrouwbaar
remain	blijven
remember	herinneren
rent vb	huren
rental	huur, de

repair *vb*	repareren
repeat	herhalen
reservation	reservering, de
reserve *vb*	reserveren
reserved	gereserveerd
rest *n (repose)*	rust, de
the rest of the wine	de rest van de wijn
rest *vb*	rusten
restaurant	restaurant, het
restaurant car	restauratiewagen, de
retire *(from work)*	met pensioen gaan
return *(go back)*	teruggaan
(give back)	teruggeven
return ticket	retour, het
reverse charge call	telefoongesprek voor rekening van de opgeroepene
rheumatism	reumatiek, de
rhubarb	rabarber, de
rice	rijst, de
rich *(person, etc.)*	rijk
(food)	vet
riding	rijden
right *adj (correct)*	goed
to be right	gelijk hebben
right	rechts
on/to the right	aan de rechterkant
turn right	ga rechtsaf
ring *n (wedding)*	ring, de
ring *vb (phone)*	opbellen
ripe	rijp
river	rivier, de
road	weg, de
road conditions	rijomstandigheden, de
road map	wegenkaart, de

road works	werkzaamheden aan de weg
roast	braden ; roosteren
robber	dief, de
roll (bread)	broodje, het
roof	dak, het
roof-rack	imperiaal, de
room (in house, hotel)	kamer, de
(space)	ruimte, de
room service	kamerbediening, de
rope	touw, het
rose	roos, de
rosé (wine)	rosé
rotten (fruit, etc.)	rot
rough (sea)	ruw
round (shape)	rond
roundabout (traffic)	rotonde, de
route	route, de
row n (line)	rij, de
row vb (boat)	roeien
rowing boat	roeiboot, de
royal	koninklijk
rubber (material)	rubber
(eraser)	gum, het
rubber band	elastiekje, het
rubbish	vuilnis, het
rucksack	rugzak, de
rudder	roer, het
rug	vloerkleed, het
ruler (measuring)	liniaal, de
rum	rum, de
run vb	hardlopen
rush hour	spitsuur, het
rusty	roestig
rye bread	roggebrood, het

sad	verdrietig
safe n	brandkast, de
safe adj	veilig
safety pin	veiligheidsspeld, de
sail vb	uitvaren
sailboat	zeilboot, de
sailing (sport)	zeilen
saint	heilige, de
salad	salade, de
salad dressing	saus, de
sale	uitverkoop, de
salesperson (female)	verkoopster, de
(male)	verkoper, de
salmon	zalm, de
salt	zout, het
same	dezelfde ; hetzelfde
sample	monster, het
sand	zand, het
sandals	sandalen, de
sandwich	sandwich, de
(toasted)	tosti, de
sanitary towels	maandverband, het
sardine	sardine, de
sauce	saus, de
saucepan	steelpan, de
saucer	schotel, de
sauna	sauna, de
sausage	worst, de
save	redden
(money)	sparen
savoury (not sweet)	hartig
say	zeggen
scallop	kammossel, de
scampi	garnalen, de

scarf *(woollen)*	das, de
(silk)	sjaal, de
school	school, de
scissors	schaar, de
score *n*	score, de
score *vb (goal)*	scoren
Scotch	Schotse whisky, de
Scotland	Schotland
Scottish	Schots
screw	schroef, de
screwdriver	schroevendraaier, de
sculpture *(object)*	beeldhouwwerk, het
sea	zee, de
seafood	vis, de
seasick	zeeziek
seaside: *at the seaside*	aan de kust
season ticket	seizoenskaart, de
seat *(chair)*	stoel, de
(in bus, train)	zitplaats, de
second	tweede
second class	tweede klas
secondhand	tweedehands
see	zien
seem	lijken
it seems to me	het lijkt me
self-service	zelfbediening
sell	verlopen
Sellotape®	plakband, het
send	sturen
senior citizen	bejaarde, de
separate	apart
serious *(accident, etc.)*	ernstig
(person)	serieus
serve	bedienen

service *(in restaurant)*	bediening, de
service charge	bedieningsgeld, het
set menu	menu, het
set off *(on journey)*	vertrekken
several	verscheidene
sew	zagen
shade	schaduw, de
shallow	laag ; ondiep
shampoo	shampoo, de
shampoo and set	wassen en krullen zetten
shandy	shandy, het
share *vb*	delen
shave	scheren
shaving cream	scheercrème, de
she	zij *see* GRAMMAR
sheep	schaap, het
sheet *(bed)*	laken, het
(paper)	blad, het
shellfish	schaaldieren, de
sherry	sherry, de
ship	schip, het
shirt	overhemd, het
shock	schok, de
shock absorber	schokdemper, de
shoe	schoen, de
shoot	schieten
shop	winkel, de
shop assistant	winkelbediende, de
shopping	winkelen
to go shopping	uit winkelen gaan
short	kort
short cut	een kortere weg
shorts	korte broek, de
shout *vb*	schreeuwen

show n	show, de
show vb	tonen
shower	douche, de
shrimp	garnaal, de
shut adj	gesloten
shut vb	sluiten
sick (ill)	ziek
side	zijkant, de
sightseeing	bekijken van bezienswaardigheden
sign n (road sign)	verkeersbord, het
sign vb	ondertekenen
signature	handtekening, de
silence	stilte, de
silk	zijde
silly	raar
silver	zilver
similar	hetzelfde
simple	simpel
sing	zingen
single (unmarried)	ongetrouwd
(not double)	enkel
single bed	éénpersoonsbed, het
single room	éénpersoonskamer, de
sink	gootsteen ,het
sir	mijnheer
sister	zuster, de
sit	zitten
size	maat, de
skates	schaatsen, de
skating	schaatsen
skimmed milk (semi)	halfvolle melk, de
skin	huid, de
sledge	slee, de

sleep *vb*	slapen
sleeper *(in train)*	slaapwagen, de
sleeping bag	slaapzak, de
sleeping car	slaapwagen, de
sleeping pill	slaappil, de
slice *(of bread)*	snee, de
(of ham)	plak, de
slide *(photograph)*	dia, de
slipper	slipper, de
slow	langzaam
small	klein
smaller	kleiner
smell *n*	reuk, de
smell *vb*	ruiken
it smells bad!	het stinkt!
smile *n*	glimlach, de
smile *vb*	glimlachen
smoke *n*	rook, de
smoke *vb*	roken
smoked	gerookt
snack bar	snackbar, de
snorkel	snorkel, de
snow *n*	sneeuw, de
snowing: *it's snowing*	het sneeuwt
so	zo
so much	zoveel
soap	zeep, de
soap powder	zeeppoeder, het ; wasmiddel, het
sober	sober ; nuchter
socket	contact, het
socks	sokken, de
soda	soda, het
soft *(not hard, smooth)*	zacht
soft drink	niet-alcoholische drank, de

some	enige ; enkele ; iets
someone	iemand
something	iets
sometimes	soms
son	zoon, de
song	lied, het
soon	gauw
sore	zeer
it's sore	*het doet zeer*
my back is sore	*mijn rug doet zeer*
sorry!	sorry!
I'm sorry!	*het spijt me!*
sort	soort, de
what sort of car?	*wat voor soort auto?*
soup	soep, de
south	zuid
souvenir	souvenir, het
space: *parking space*	parkeerplaats, de
spade	schop, de
spanner	moersleutel, de
(adjustable)	engelse sleutel, de
spare wheel	reservewiel, het
sparkling	sprankelend
spark plug	bougie, de
speak	spreken
special	speciaal
speciality	specialiteit, de
speed	snelheid, de
speed limit	snelheidslimiet, de
spell *vb*	spellen
how is it spelt?	*hoe wordt het gespeld?*
spicy	pikant
spinach	spinazie, de
spirit *(ghost)*	geest, de

spirits (*drink*)	sterke drank, de
spit *vb*	spuwen
sponge	spons, de
spoon	lepel, de
sport	sport, de
sprained	verstuikt
spring (*season*)	lente, de
square (*in town*)	plein, het
squash (*game*)	squash
squid	(pijl-)inktvis, de
stairs	trap, de
stalls (*theatre*)	stalles, de
stamp (*postage*)	postzegel, de
star	ster, de
start (*car*)	starten
starter (*in meal*)	voorgerecht, het
(*in car*)	contact, het
station	station, het
stationer's	kantoorboekhandel, de
stay (*remain*)	blijven
I'm staying at ...	*ik verblijf in ...*
steak	biefstuk, de
steamer (*boat*)	stoomboot, de
steep	stijl
is it steep?	*is het stijl?*
steering wheel	stuurwiel, het
sterling (*pounds*)	Britse pond, het
stew	stoofpot, de
steward (*on plane*)	steward, de
stewardess (*on plane*)	stewardess, de
sticking plaster	pleister, de
sting n	beet, de
sting vb	bijten
stockings	kousen, de

stomach	maag, de ; buik, de
my stomach is upset	*mijn maag is van streek*
stone	steen, de
stop	stop
stopover	onderbreking, de
storey	verdieping, de
storm	storm, de
straight on	rechtdoor
strange	vreemd
straw (for drinking)	rietje, het
strawberry	aardbei, de
street	straat, de
street map	plattegrond, de
strike	staking, de
string	touwtje, het
striped	gestreept
strong	sterk
struggle	worstelen
stuck	vast
it's stuck	*het zit vast*
student	student, de
stung	steken
stupid	dom
suddenly	opeens
suede	suède, het
sugar	suiker, de
suit n	kostuum, het ; pak, het
suit vb	schikken
it doesn't suit me	*het schikt me niet*
suitcase	koffer, de
summer	zomer, de
sun	zon, de
sunbathe	zonnebaden
sunburn	zonnebrand

sunglasses	zonnebril, de
sunny	zonnig
it's sunny	*het is zonnig*
sunshade	zonnewering, de
sunstroke	zonnesteek, de
suntanned	gebruind
suntan lotion	zonnebrandlotion, de
supermarket	supermarkt, de
supplement *(train, etc.)*	toeslag, de
sure	zeker
surfboard	surfplank, de
surname	achternaam, de
surprise	verrassing, de
surrounded by	omgeven door
swallow *vb*	slikken
sweat *n*	zweet, het
sweater	trui, de
sweatshirt	sweatshirt, het
sweet *adj*	zoet
sweet *n (dessert)*	nagerecht, het
sweetener	zoetmaker, de
sweets	snoep, het
swim	zwemmen
swimming pool	zwembad, het
swimsuit	zwempak, het
swing *(children's)*	schommel, de
switch	schakelaar, de
switch off	uitdoen
switch on	aandoen
swollen	gezwollen
synagogue	synagoge, de

table	tafel, de
tablecloth	tafellaken, het ; tafelkleed, het
tablespoon	eetlepel, de
tablet	tablet, het
table wine	tafelwijn, de
tail	staart, de
tailor's	kleermaker, de
take (medicine, etc.)	nemen
how long does it take?	hoelang duurt het?
take out	meenemen
talc	talk, de
talk	praten
tall	lang
tame	tam
tampons	tampons, de
tap	kraan, de
tape (music)	geluidscassette, de
tape-recorder	cassetterecorder, de ; bandrecorder, de
taste vb	proeven
can I taste it?	mag ik het proeven?
taste n	smaak, de
tax n	belasting, de
taxi	taxi, de
taxi driver	taxichauffeur, de
taxi rank	taxistandplaats, de
tea	thee, de
teabag	theezakje, het
teach	leren
teacher (male)	leraar, de
(female)	lerares, de
team	team, het
teapot	theepot, de

tear (crying)	traan, de
(in material)	scheur, de
teaspoon	theelepel, de
teat (on baby's bottle)	speen, de
teeshirt	T-shirt, het
teeth	tanden, de
telephone	telefoon, de
telephone box	telefooncel, de
telephone call	telefoongesprek, het
telephone directory	telefoonboek, het
television	televisie, de
telex	telex, de
tell	vertellen
I will tell him	*ik zal hem vertellen*
temperature	temperatuur, de
I have a temperature	*ik heb koorts*
temporary	tijdelijk
tennis	tennis
tennis ball	tennisbal, de
tennis court	tennisveld, het
tennis racket	tennisracket, het
tent	tent, de
tent peg	haring, de
terminus	eindpunt, het
terrace	terras, het
text	tekst, de
than	dan
more than	*meer dan*
less than	*minder dan*
thank you	dank u
thanks very much	*dank u wel*
that	die ; dat
that book	*dat boek*
that table	*die tafel*
that one	*dat*

thaw: *it's thawing*	*het dooit*
theatre	theater, het
then	toen
(afterwards)	daarna
there	daar
there is/there are	*er is/er zijn*
therefore	daarom
thermometer	thermometer, de
these	deze
they	zij *see* **GRAMMAR**
thick	dik
thief	dief, de
thigh	dij, de
thin	dun
thing	ding, het
my things	*mijn spullen*
think	denken
(be of opinion)	van mening zijn
third	derde
thirsty	dorstig
I'm thirsty	*ik heb dorst*
this	deze ; dit
this book	*dit boek*
this table	*deze tafel*
those	die
thread	draad, de
throat	keel, de
throat lozenge	keeltablet, het
through	door
thunder	donder, de
thunderstorm	onweersbui, de
ticket	kaartje, het
ticket collector	conducteur, de ; controleur, de
ticket office	kaartverkoop, de

tide	getijde, het
tie	stropdas, de
tights	panties, de ; nylons, de
till (cash)	kassa, de
till prep	tot
time	tijd, de
for the first time	voor de eerste keer
this time	deze keer
what time is it?	hoe laat is het?
timetable	dienstregeling, de
tin	blik, het
tinfoil	zilverpapier, het
tin-opener	blikopener, de
tip n (to waiter, etc.)	fooi, de
tired	moe
tissues	papieren zakdoekjes, de
to	naar ; tot ; voor
toast	toast, de
tobacco	tabak, de
tobacconist's	sigarenwinkel, de
today	vandaag
a week today	over een week
together	samen
toilet	toilet, het
toilet paper	toiletpapier, het
toll	tol, de
tomato	tomaat, de
tomato juice	tomatensap, het
tomorrow	morgen
tomorrow morning	morgenochtend
tomorrow afternoon	morgenmiddag
tongue	tong, de
tonic water	tonic, de
tonight	vannacht

too (also)	ook
too big	*te groot*
too small	*te klein*
tooth	tand, de
(molar)	kies, de
toothache	kiespijn, de
toothbrush	tandenborstel, de
toothpaste	tandpasta, de
toothpick	tandestoker, de
top adj	hoogste
the top floor	*de bovenste verdieping*
top n (of hill)	top, de
on top of ...	*boven op ...*
torch	zaklamp, de
torn	gescheurd
total	totaal, het
tough (meat)	stug
tour (trip)	tour, de
(of museum, etc.)	rondleiding, de
tourist	toerist, de
tourist office	VVV ; tourist information, de
tourist ticket	toeristenkaart, de
tow vb	slepen
towel	handdoek, de
tower	toren, de
town	stad, de
town centre	centrum, het
town hall	stadhuis, het
town plan	plattegrond, de
tow rope	sleepkabel, de
toy	speelgoed, het
tracksuit	trainingspak, het
tradition	traditie, de
traditional	traditioneel

traffic	verkeer, het
traffic lights	verkeerslichten, de
trailer	aanhanger, de
train	trein, de
by train	*per trein*
training shoes	trainingsschoenen, de
tram	tram, de
translate	vertalen
translation	vertaling, de
travel	reizen
travel agent	reisbureau, het
traveller's cheque	travellercheque, de
tray	dienblad, het
tree	boom, de
trip	reis, de
trolley	wagentje, het
trouble	moeilijkheden, de
trousers	broek, de
trout	forel, de
true	waar
trunk *(luggage)*	hutkoffer, de
trunks *(swimming)*	zwembroek, de
truth	waarheid, de
try *(attempt)*	proberon
try on *(clothes)*	proberen
tuna	tonijn, de
tunnel	tunnel, de
turkey	kalkoen, de
turn	draaien
turn left/right	*ga linksaf/rechtsaf*
turnip	knolraap, de
turn off *(light, etc.)*	uitdoen
(tap)	dichtdraaien
(engine)	afdoen

turn on (light, etc.)	aandoen
(tap)	opendraaien
tweezers	tangetje, het ; pincet, het
twice	twee keer
twin-bedded room	dubbele kamer
type vb	typen
typical	typisch
tyre	band, de
tyre pressure	luchtdruk, de

umbrella	paraplu, de
uncle	oom, de
uncomfortable	oncomfortabel
unconscious	bewusteloos
under	onder
underground (metro)	metro, de
underpants	onderbroek, de
underpass	onderdoorgang, de
understand (meaning)	begrijpen
I don't understand you	ik versta je niet
underwear	ondergoed, het
unemployed	werkloos
unfasten	losmaken
unhappy	ongelukkig
United States	Verenigde Staten, de
university	universiteit, de
unleaded petrol	loodvrije benzine, de
unpack	uitpakken
I have to unpack	ik moet uitpakken
unscrew	losschroeven
up	op ; boven
(out of bed)	uit bed
upside down	ondersteboven

upstairs	boven
urgent	dringend
urine	urine, de
USA	VS (Verenigde Staten van Amerika)
use	gebruiken
used to	gevend aan
I'm used to...	ik ben gewend aan...
useful	nuttig
usual	gewoon ; gebruikelijk
my usual drink, please	mijn gewone drankje, alstublieft
usually	gewoonlijk
U-turn (to make)	(om)keren

vacancies (in hotel)	kamers beschikbaar, de ; kamers vrij, de
vacuum cleaner	stofzuiger, de
valid	geldig
valley	vallei, de
valuable	kostbaar ; waardevol
valuables	kostbaarheden, de
van	bestelauto, de
(camper)	kampeerauto, de
vase	vaas, de
VAT	BTW
veal	kalfsvlees, het
vegetables	groente, de
vegetarian (person)	vegetariër, de
vegetarian	vegetarisch
vein	ader, de
velvet	fluweel, het
ventilator	ventilator, de

vermouth	vermouth, de
very	zeer, erg
vest	hemd, het
via	via
video	video, de
video camera	videocamera, de
view (panorama)	uitzicht, het
villa	villa, de
village	dorp, het
vinegar	azijn, de
visa	visum, het
visit vb	bezoeken
vitamin	vitamine, de
vodka	wodka, de
voice	stem, de
voltage	voltage
wage	loon, het
waist	middel, de
wait for	wachten op
waiter	ober, de ; kelner, de
waiting room	wachtkamer, de
waitress	serveerster, de
Wales	Wales
walk vb	lopen ; wandelen
walk n	wandeling, de
to go for a walk	*gaan wandelen*
walking stick	wandelstok, de
wall (outside)	muur, de
(inside)	wand, de
wallet	portefeuille, de
walnut	walnoot, de
want vb	willen

war	oorlog, de
warm	warm
it's warm (weather)	*het is warm*
warning triangle	gevarendriehoek, de
wash	wassen
(wash oneself)	zich wassen
washbasin	waskom, de
washing machine	wasmachine, de
washing powder	waspoeder, het
washing-up liquid	afwasmiddel, het
wasp	wesp, de
waste vb (money)	verkwisten
(time)	verspillen
waste bin	vuilnisbak, de
watch n	horloge, het
watch vb (look at)	kijken (naar)
watchstrap	horlogebandje, het
water	water, het
waterfall	waterval, de
water heater	boiler, de ; geiser, de
watermelon	watermeloen, de
waterproof	waterproef
water-skiing	waterskiën
wave (on sea)	golf, de
wax	was, de
way (manner)	manier, de
(route)	weg, de
we	wij, we
weak (person)	zwak
(coffee)	slap
wear	dragen
weather	weer, het
wedding	huwelijk, het
week	week, de

weekday	werkdag, de
weekend	weekeinde, het
weight	gewicht, het
welcome	welkom
well	goed
he's not well	*hij voelt zich niet goed*
well-done *(steak)*	doorgebakken
Welsh	Wels
west	west
wet	nat
what?	wat?
what is it?	*wat is dit?*
wheel	wiel, het
wheelchair	rolstoel, de
when	als ; wanneer
when?	*wanneer?*
where *conj.*	waar
where?	*waar?*
which	welke
which is it?	*welke is het?*
which hotel?	*welk hotel?*
which table?	*welke tafel?*
while	terwijl
in a short while	*over een poosje*
whisky	whisky, de
white	wit
who: *who is it?*	*wie is het?*
whole	heel
wholemeal bread	volkorenbrood, het
whose: *whose is it?*	*van wie is het*
why?	waarom?
wide	wijd
wife	echtgenote, de ; vrouw, de
wind	wind, de
windmill	windmolen, de

window	raam, het ; venster, het
(shop)	etalage, de
(ticket office)	loket, het
(in car, train)	raampje, het
windscreen (car)	voorruit, de
(back window)	achterruit, de
windsurfing	windsurfen
windy	winderig
it's windy	het waait
wine	wijn, de
wine list	wijnlijst, de
winter	winter, de
with	met
without	zonder
woman	vrouw, de
wood (material)	hout, het
(forest)	bos, het
wool	wol, de
work vb	werken
worried	bezorgd
worse	slechter
worth: it's worth ...	het is ... waard
wrap up (parcel, etc.)	inpakken
wrapping paper	inpakpapier, het
write	schrijven
writing paper	schrijfpapier, het
wrong (incorrect)	fout ; verkeerd
what's wrong?	wat is er aan de hand?
X-rays	röntgenstralen, de

yacht	jacht, het
year	jaar, het
yellow	geel
yes	ja ; jawel
yes, please	*ja, alstublieft*
yesterday	gisteren
yet	nog
not yet	*nog niet*
yoghurt	yoghurt, de
you *(polite sing.)*	u
(polite plural)	u
(sing. with friends)	jij ; je
(plural with friends)	jullie
young	jong
youth hostel	jeugdherberg, de
zero	nul
zip	ritssluiting, de
zoo	dierentuin, de

aal, de	eel
aambeien, de	haemorrhoids
aan	on *(light, TV)*
aan de beurt?	when is it due?
aanbevelen	recommend
aanbod, het	offer
aandoen	to switch on *(light, etc.)*
aandrijfsnaar, de	fan belt
aangeven	to declare
aanhanger, de	trailer
aank.	arrival *(abbreviation)*
aankomen	to arrive
aankomst, de	arrival
aankondiging, de	notice *(sign)*
aanproberen	to try on *(clothes)*
aanraken	to touch
niet aanraken	do not touch
aansluiting, de	connection *(train, etc.)*
aansteken	to light
aansteker, de	lighter
aantrekkelijk	attractive *(person)*
aap, de	monkey
aardbeving, de	earthquake
aardappel, de	potato
aardbei, de	strawberry
aarde, de	earth
aardewerk, het	pottery
aardig	kind ; nice
abdij, de	abbey
abrikoos, de	apricot
accu, de	battery
achter	behind
achterlaten	to leave *(behind)*
achternaam, de	surname

achterruit, de	back window
actueel	current
ademhalen	to breathe
ader, de	vein
adres, het	address
adresboek, het	directory
advertentie, de	advertisement
advies, het	advice
adviseren,	to advise
advocaat, de	lawyer ; Dutch drink based on egg yolks
afdoen	to turn off (engine)
afgeprijsd	reduced
afmaken	to finish
afspraak, de	appointment
after-shave, de	aftershave
afwasmachine, de	dishwasher
afwasmiddel, het	washing-up liquid
afzender, de	sender
agent, de	policeman ; agent
agentschap, het	agency
airconditioning, de	air-conditioning
aktentas, de	briefcase
al	already
alarm, het	alarm
alcohol, de	alcohol
alcoholisch	alcoholic
algemene feestdag, de	public holiday
alle	all ; every
allebei	both
alleen	alone
alleen	just
alleen twee	just two

allergisch voor	**allergic to**
alles	**everything**
als	**when ; if**
alsjeblieft	**please** *(informal)*
alstublieft	**please** *(formal, polite)*
altijd	**always**
amandel, de	**almond**
ambassade, de	**embassy**
ambulance, de	**ambulance**
Amerika	**America**
Amerikaan	**American** *(person)*
Amerikaans	**American**
amusement, het	**entertainments**
ananas, de	**pineapple**
ander	**other**
de andere	**the other one**
anders niets	**nothing else**
anders niets?	**anything else?**
annuleren	**to cancel**
antibiotisch	**antibiotic**
antiseptisch	**antiseptic**
antivriesmiddel, het	**antifreeze**
antwoord, het	**answer**
antwoorden	**to answer**
apart	**separate**
aperitief, het	**apéritif**
appartement, het	**apartment**
appel, de	**apple**
appelwijn, de	**cider**
april	**April**
archief, het	**archives ; computer file**
arm, de	**arm**
armband, de	**bracelet**
arresteren	**to arrest**

artisjok, de	artichoke
asbak, de	ashtray
asperge, de	asparagus
aspirine, de	aspirin
astma, de	asthma
a.u.b	please (abbreviation)
aubergine, de	aubergine
augustus	August
Australië	Australia
Australiër	Australian (person)
Australisch	Australian
auteur, de	author
auto, de	car
autobus, de	bus
automatisch	automatic
autopech, het	breakdown (car)
autosleutel, de	ignition key (car)
autoveerboot, de	car ferry
autoweg, de	motorway
avocado, de	avocado
avond, de	evening
's avonds	in the evening
avondeten, het	evening meal
azijn, de	vinegar
B-weg, de	minor road
baan, de	job
baas, de	boss
baby, de	baby
babyvoeding, de	baby food
bacon, het	bacon
bad, het	bath

badkamer, de	bathroom
badmuts, de	bathing cap
bagage ophalen	baggage reclaim
bagage, de	luggage
bagagelabel, de	luggage tag
bagagenet, het	luggage rack
bagagerek, het	luggage rack
bagageruimte, de	car trunk
bagagewagentje, het	luggage trolley
bakker, de	baker's
bal, de	ball
balie, de	(check-in) desk
balkon, het	balcony
banaan, de	banana
band, de	band *(musical)* ; tyre
bandrecorder, de	tape-recorder
bang	frightened
bank, de	bank
bar, de	bar
batterij, de	battery
bed, het	bed
beddegoed, het	bedding
bedelaar, de	beggar
bedienen	to serve
bedieningsgeld, het	service charge
bediening, de	service *(in restaurant)*
bedorven	off *(fruit and vegetables)*
bedrijf, het	business *(company)*
beeldhouwwerk, het	sculpture *(object)*
been, het	bone ; leg
beet, de	bite ; sting
beetje: een beetje	a bit ; a little
beginnen	to begin

begraafplaats, de	cemetery
begrafenis, de	funeral
begrijpen	to understand *(meaning)*
beha, de	bra
behalve	except
beide	either
bejaarde, de	senior citizen
bekneld	jammed
bel, de	bell
belangrijk	important
belangrijkste	main ; most important
belasting, de	tax
belastingvrije winkel, de	duty-free shop
bellen	press the bell *(sign)*
beneden	down ; below
benedenverdieping, de	ground floor
bent u in orde?	are you all right?
benzine, de	petrol
benzinestation, het	petrol station
beoordelen	to judge
berg, de	mountain
beroemd	famous
beroven	to rob
besmettelijk	infectious
beste	best
bestek, het	cutlery
bestelauto, de	van
bestellen	to order
bestelling, de	order *(in pub)*
bestuurder, de	driver *(of car)*
betaald	paid
betalen	to pay
betaling, de	payment

betekenen	**to mean** (*signify*)
beter	**better**
betrouwbaar	**reliable** (*method*)
bevatten	**to contain**
bevestigen	**to confirm**
bewegen	**to move**
bewolkt	**cloudy**
bewusteloos	**unconscious**
bezem, de	**broom**
bezet	**occupied** (*toilet*) ; **engaged** (*phone*)
bezoeken	**to visit**
bezorgd	**worried**
bibliotheek, de	**library**
biefstuk, de	**steak**
bier, het	**beer ; lager**
bij	**at ; near**
bijbetaling, de	**supplement** (*on train, etc.*)
bijna	**almost**
bijsluiten	**to enclose**
bijten	**to bite ; to sting**
bijvoorbeeld	**for example**
bikini, de	**bikini**
binnen	**indoors**
binnenbad	**indoor swimming pool**
binnengaan	**to go in**
binnenkomen	**to enter**
bioscoop, de	**cinema**
biscuitje, het	**biscuit**
bitter	**bitter**
blaar, de	**blister**
blad, het	**leaf ; sheet** (*paper*)
bladzijde, de	**page**
blaffen	**to bark** (*dog*)

blauw	**blue**
bleek	**pale**
bleekmiddel, het	**bleach**
blijven	**to remain ; to stay**
blik, het	**can ; tin**
blikopener, de	**tin-opener**
blinde	**blind** *(person)*
blindedarmontsteking, de	**appendicitis**
blocnote, de	**note pad**
bloed, het	**blood**
bloedgroep, de	**blood group**
bloem, de	**flower ; flour**
bloemkool, de	**cauliflower**
blond	**blond ; fair** *(hair)*
blouse, de	**blouse**
boek, het	**book**
boeken	**to book**
boekwinkel, de	**bookshop**
boer, de	**farmer**
boerderij, de	**farm**
boete, de	**fine** *(to be paid)*
bof, de	**mumps**
boiler, de	**boiler ; water heater**
bol, de	**bulb** *(flower)*
bollenveld, het	**bulb field**
bont	**fur**
boodschap, de	**message**
boom, de	**tree**
boomgaard, de	**orchard**
boon, de	**bean**
boos	**angry**
boot, de	**boat**
boottocht, de	**boat trip**

bord, het	**dish ; plate ; sign**
borst, de	**breast** (chicken)
borstel, de	**brush**
bos, het	**wood** (forest)
boter, de	**butter**
bougie, de	**spark plug ; points** (in car)
boven	**above ; upstairs ; over**
bovenop	**on top of**
bovenste	**top**
braden	**roast**
brand!	**fire!**
brandblusser, de	**fire extinguisher**
branden	**to burn**
brandkast, de	**safe**
brandstof, de	**fuel**
brandweer, de	**fire brigade**
breekbaar	**breakable**
breien	**knit**
breken	**to break**
brengen	**to bring ; to fetch**
breuk, de	**fracture**
bridge	**bridge** (game)
brief, de	**letter**
briefje, het	**note ; bank note**
briefkaart, de	**postcard**
brievenbus, de	**letterbox**
bril, de	**glasses** (spectacles)
Brits	**British**
Britse pond, het	**sterling** (pound)
broche, de	**brooch**
brochure, de	**brochure**
broek, de	**trousers**
broer, de	**brother**

brood, het	bread ; loaf
broodje, het	bun ; bread roll
brug, de	bridge
bruin	brown
BTW	VAT
buigtang, de	pliers
buik, de	stomach
buiten	outside
buitenbad	outdoor poor
buitenlands	foreign
buitenwijken, de	outskirts ; suburbs
bus, de	bus ; coach
bushalte, de	bus stop
buskaartje, het	bus ticket
busstation, het	bus station
bustocht, de	bus tour ; coach trip
buur, de	neighbour
cabaret, het	cabaret
cacao, de	cocoa
cadeau, het	gift ; present
cadeauwinkel, de	gift shop
café, het	café *(bar)*
cake, de	cake
camcorder, de	camcorder
camera, de	camera
camping, de	campsite
Canada	Canada
Canadees	Canadian
caravan, de	caravan
carburateur, de	carburettor
casino, het	casino

centimeter	centimetre
centrum, het	centre ; town centre
certificaat, het	certificate
champagne, de	champagne
champignon, de	mushroom
cheque, de	cheque
chequeboek, het	cheque book
chequepas, de	cheque card
chips, de	crisps
chocolaatjes, de	chocolates
chocolade, de	chocolate
chocolademelk, de	drinking chocolate
circus, het	circus
citroen, de	lemon
citroenthee, de	lemon tea
cliënt, de	client
club, de	club
Coca Cola®	Coke®
cocktail, de	cocktail
coffeeshop, de	coffeeshop
cognac, de	brandy
communie, de	communion
compartiment, het	compartment
computer, de	computer
concert, het	concert
conditioner, de	conditioner
condoom, het	condom
conducteur, de	conductor *(on bus)* ; ticket collector
conferentie, de	conference
consulaat, het	consulate
contact, het	socket ; ignition *(car)*
contactlens-schoon-maakmiddel, het	contact lens cleaner

contactlenzen, de	contact lenses
contact opnemen met	to contact
contant	cash
controleren	to check
controleur, de	guard (on train)
conversatiezaal, de	lounge (in hotel)
coupé, de	train compartment
courgettes, de	courgettes
couvert, het	cover charge
creditcard, de	credit card
crème, de	cream (lotion)
cruise, de	cruise

daar	there
daarna	afterwards
daarom	therefore
dag	goodbye
dag!	cheerio!
dag, de	day
dagboek, het	diary
dagelijks	daily
dagkart, de	day ticket (public transport, etc.)
dak, het	roof
dame, de	lady
dames	ladies (toilet)
damesonderbroek, de	panties
dampen, de	fumes
dan	than
dank je/u	thank you (informal/formal)
dank je/u wel	thank you very much (informal/formal)
dans, de	dance
dansen	to dance

das, de	**scarf** (woollen)
dat	**that**
datum, de	**date**
de	**the**
de heer (dhr)	**Mr**
december	**December**
deel, het	**part**
Deens	**Danish**
defect	**out of order** (sign)
dekbed, het	**duvet**
deken, de	**blanket ; quilt**
deksel, het	**lid**
dekstoel, de	**deck chair**
delen	**to share**
Denemarken	**Denmark**
denken	**to think**
deodorant, de	**deodorant**
deposito, de	**deposit**
derde	**third**
details, de	**details**
deur, de	**door**
deuren sluiten	**close the doors** (sign)
deze	**these**
deze keer	**this time**
dezelfde	**same**
dia, de	**slide** (photograph)
diamant, de	**diamond**
diarree, de	**diarrhoea**
dicht	**shut ; closed** (sign)
dichtdraaien	**to close** (tap)
die	**that ; those**
dieet, het	**diet**
dief, de	**thief ; robber**

dienblad, het	tray
dienstregeling, de	timetable
diep	deep
diepvries, de	deep freeze ; frozen food
dier, het	animal
dierentuin, de	zoo
diesel	diesel
dij, de	thigh
dik	thick
diner, het	dinner
dineren	to have dinner
ding, het	thing
direct	at once
directeur, de	director (company)
disco, de	disco
dit	this
dochter, de	daughter
document, het	document
doden	kill
doek, de	cloth (rag)
doen	to do
dokter, de	doctor
dollar, de	dollar
dom	stupid
dominee, de	minister (church)
donder, de	thunder
donker	dark
donut, de	doughnut
dood	dead
dooi	thaw
door	through
doorgebakken	well done (steak)
doos, de	box

doperwten, de	peas
dorp, het	village
dorst, de	thirst
douane, de	customs *(at border)*
douche, de	shower
dozijn	dozen
draad, de	thread ; lead *(electric)*
draaien	to turn ; to dial
dragen	to carry ; wear
drank, de	drink
dringend	urgent
drinken	to drink
drinkwater, het	drinking water
drogen	to dry
drogist, de	chemist's
dronken	drunk
droog	dry
druiven, de	grapes
druk	busy ; crowded
dubbel	double
dubbelspel, het	doubles *(tennis)*
duidelijk	obvious
duiken	to dive
duiker, de	diver
Duits	German
Duitsland	Germany
duizelig	dizzy
dun	thin
duur	expensive
duwen	to push ; push *(sign)*
dynamo, de	dynamo

eb, de	low tide
echt	genuine ; real
echtgenoot, de	husband
echtgenote, de	wife
editie, de	edition
een	a
één	one
eend, de	duck
éénpersoonsbed, het	single bed
éénpersoonskamer, de	single room
éénrichtingsverkeer	one-way traffic
eens	once
eergisteren	the day before yesterday
eerste	first
eerste hulp	first aid
eerste klas, de	first class
eerste verdieping, de	first floor
eetkamer, de	dining room
eetlepel, de	tablespoon
eeuw, de	century
EHBO	first-aid post (sign)
ei, het	egg
eieren, de	eggs
eigenaar, de	owner
eik, de	oak
eiland, het	island
einde, het	end
eindigen	to finish ; to end
eindpunt, het	terminus
elastiek, het	elastic
elastiekje, het	rubber band
elektricien, de	electrician
elektriciteit, de	electricity

elektriciteitsmeter, de	electricity meter
elektrisch	electric
electronisch	electronic
emmer, de	bucket
en	and
Engeland	England
Engels	English
Engelse, de	English woman
Engelsman, de	Englishman
engelse sleutel, de	adjustable spanner
enig	only *(child)*
enige	some
enkel	single *(not double)*
enkele	a few
enkele reis, de	single journey *(train, etc.)*
enkelspel, het	singles *(tennis)*
enthousiast	enthusiastic
envelop, de	envelope
er	there
er is een misverstand	there's been a misunderstanding
er is/er zijn	there is/there are
erg	very
ernstig	serious *(accident, etc.)*
essentieel	essential
etalage, de	shop window
eten	to eat
etiket, het	label
Eurocheque, de	Eurocheque
Europa	Europe
Europees	European
Europese Unie, de	European Union
examen, het	examination
excursie, de	excursion

expert, de	**expert**
expres	**on purpose**
exprespost	**express post**
extra	**extra**
f.	**price in Dutch guilders**
fabriceren	**to manufacture**
fabriek, de	**factory**
faciliteiten, de	**facilities**
factuur, de	**invoice**
familie, de	**family** (large)
fan, de	**fan** (cinema, jazz, etc.)
favoriet	**favourite**
februari	**February**
feest, het	**party** (celebration)
fiets, de	**bicycle**
fietsen	**to cycle**
fietspad, het	**cycle path**
fietspomp, de	**bicycle pump**
fietstas, de	**bicycle bag**
fietstocht, de	**cycle tour**
fietsverhuur	**cycle hire** (sign)
file, het	**file** (cumputer)
filet	**fillet**
film, de	**film** (at cinema, for camera)
filter, het	**filter**
fit	**fit** (healthy)
fl.	**price in Dutch guilders**
flat, de	**flat** (apartment)
flauw	**faint**
flauwgevallen	**fainted**
fles, de	**bottle**

flessenopener, de	**bottle opener**
flippers, de	**flippers**
fluitketel, de	**kettle**
fluweel, het	**velvet**
folie, de	**foil**
fontein, de	**fountain**
fooi, de	**tip** (to waiter, etc.)
forel, de	**trout**
formulier, het	**form** (document)
foto, de	**photograph**
fotograferen	**to photograph**
fotokopie, de	**photocopy**
fotokopiëren	**to photocopy**
fout, de	**mistake**
fout	**wrong** (incorrect)
framboos, de	**raspberry**
franje, de	**fringe**
Frankrijk	**France**
Frans	**French**
fruit, het	**fruit**
gaan	**to go**
ga linksaf	**turn left**
ga rechtsaf	**turn right**
gallerie, de	**art gallery**
gallerij, de	**gallery**
gang, de	**course** (of meal) ; **aisle**
gangpad, het	**aisle**
gans, de	**goose**
garage, de	**garage**
garantie, de	**guarantee**
garderobe, de	**cloakroom**
garnaal, de	**prawn ; shrimp**

gas, het	gas
gashouder, de	gas cylinder
gast, de	guest
gat, het	hole
gauw	soon
gebak, het	cake
gebakken	fried
gebakken ei	fried egg
gebeuren	to happen
geblesseerd	injured *(sport)*
geblokkeerd	blocked *(road, pipe)*
geboorte, de	birth
geboortedatum, de	date of birth
gebouw, het	building
gebraden	roast
gebroken	broken
gebruiken	to use
gebruind	suntanned
gedetailleerd	detailed
gedistilleerd water	distilled water
gedurende	during
geel	yellow
geelzucht, de	jaundice
geen	none ; not any
geen ingang	no entry *(sign)*
geen uitgang	no exit *(sign)*
gegrild	grilled
gehakt, het	mince ; chopped
gehandicapt	handicapped
geheel	completely
geiser, de	water boiler
geit, de	goat
geitje, het	kid *(young goat)*
gek	mad

gekookt	boiled
gekookt ei	boiled egg
gelatine-pudding, de	jelly (dessert)
geld, het	cash ; money
geld inwerpen	insert coins (sign)
geld terug	change
gepast geld	exact fare (on buses, etc.)
geldig	valid
geleden	ago ; suffered
gelijk	even ; right ; correct
gelijk hebben	to be right
geloven	to believe
geluidscassette, de	cassette ; tape (music)
gelukkig	happy ; lucky
geluk hebben	to be lucky
gelukwensen!	congratulations!
gemakkelijk	easy
gember, de	ginger
geneesmiddel, het	drug (medicinal)
genieten	to enjoy
genoeg	enough
gepensioneerde, de	pensioner
geperst	squeezed
geperste sinaasappel	fresh orange juice
geregistreerd	registered
gereserveerd	reserved
gerieflijk	comfortable
gerookt	smoked
geroosterd	grilled
gescheiden	divorced
gescheurd	torn
gesloten	closed ; shut
geest, de	ghost
gestoofd	stewed

gestreept	**striped**
getijde, het	**tide**
getrouwd	**married**
gevaar	**danger** *(sign)*
gevaarlijk	**dangerous**
gevarendriehoek, de	**warning triangle** *(car)*
geven	**to give**
gevonden voorwerpen	**lost property** *(sign)*
gewend aan	**used to**
ik ben gewend aan...	**I'm used to...**
gewicht, het	**weight**
gewond	**injured**
gewoon	**usual**
gewoonlijk	**usually**
gewoonten, de	**customs**
gewricht, het	**joint** *(bone)*
gezelschap, het	**company**
gezicht, het	**face**
gezin, het	**family** *(small)*
gezwollen	**swollen**
gids, de	**guide**
giftig	**poisonous**
gisteren	**yesterday**
glas, het	**glass** *(for drinking, substance)*
glascontainer, de	**bottle bank**
glimlach, de	**smile**
glimlachen	**to smile**
gloeilamp, de	**light bulb**
glucose, de	**glucose**
goed	**good ; all right ; well**
goedemiddag	**good afternoon**
goedemorgen	**good morning**
goedenacht	**good night**
goedenavond	**good evening**

goedkoop	cheap
goedkoper	cheaper
gokken	gambling
golf	golf
golf, de	wave (on sea)
golfbaan, de	golf course
gootsteen, het	sink
goud, het	gold
gracht, de	canal (in town)
gram, het	gramme
grap, de	joke
grapefruit, de	grapefruit
gras, het	grass
gratis	free
grens, de	border
griep, de	flu
grijs	grey
groen	green
groente, de	vegetables
groep, de	group ; party
grond, de	ground
grondzeil, het	groundsheet
groot	big ; large ; tall ; great
Groot Brittannië	Great Britain
grootmoeder, de	grandmother
grootvader, de	grandfather
grot, de	cave
groter	bigger
gulden, de	Dutch guilder
gum, het	eraser
gymschoenen, de	gym shoes

haar	her
haar, het	hair
haarborstel, de	hairbrush
haardroger, de	hairdryer
haarspeld, de	hairgrip
haast	hurry
ik heb haast	I'm in a hurry
hairspray, de	hair spray
halen	to fetch ; to bring ; to get
half	half
halfvolle melk, de	semi-skimmed milk
hallo	hello
halssnoer, het	necklace
ham, de	ham
hand, de	hand
handbagage, de	hand luggage
handdoek, de	towel
handschoenen, de	gloves
handtas, de	handbag
handtekening, de	signature
hangslot, het	padlock
hard	hard ; loud
hardgekookt ei	hard-boiled egg
hardlopen	to jog ; to run
haring, de	herring ; tent peg
hart, het	heart
hartaanval, de	heart attack
hartelijke!	congratulations!
hartig	savoury *(not sweet)*
haven, de	harbour ; port *(seaport)*
haver, de	oats
hazelnoot, de	hazelnut
hebben	to have
heel	whole ; quite

heer, de	**gentleman**
heerlijk	**delicious**
heet	**hot**
heilige, de	**saint**
helling, de	**ramp**
help!	**help!**
helpen	**to help**
hemd, het	**vest**
hengel, de	**fishing rod**
heren	**gents** *(toilets)*
herfst, de	**autumn**
herhalen	**to repeat**
herinneren	**to remember**
herkennen	**to recognize**
het	**the ; it**
hetzelfde	**similar**
heuvel, de	**hill**
hier	**here**
hij	**he**
hoe	**how** *(in what way)*
hoed, de	**hat**
hoek, de	**corner**
hoelang	**how long**
hoest, de	**cough**
hoesttabletten, de	**cough sweets**
hoeveel?	**how much? ; how many?**
hoge bloeddruk	**high blood pressure**
hoi	**hi** *(informal greeting)*
Holland	**Holland**
hond, de	**dog**
hondsdolheid, de	**rabies**
hongerig	**hungry**
honing, de	**honey**

hoofd, het	head
hoofdgerecht, het	main course
hoofdpijn, de	headache
hoog	high
hooikoorts, de	hay fever
hopen	to hope
horen	to hear
horloge, het	watch (on wrist)
horlogebandje, het	watchstrap
hotel, het	hotel
houden	to hold ; to keep
houden van	to like ; to love
hout, het	wood (material)
hovercraft, de	hovercraft
huid, de	skin
huis, het	house ; home
huiswijn, de	house wine
hulp, de	help
huren	to hire ; to rent
hutkoffer, de	trunk (luggage)
huur, de	rent
te huur	to let (for rent)
huwelijk, het	wedding
huwelijksreis, de	honeymoon
ieder	any ; each ; every
iedereen	everyone
iemand	someone
Ierland	Ireland
Iers	Irish
iets	something
ijs, het	ice ; ice cream

ijsbaan, de	ice rink
ijslolly, de	ice lolly
ijzel, de	black ice
ijzer, het	iron
ijzerwarenhandel, de	ironmonger's
ik	I
imperiaal, de	roof-rack
in	in ; inside ; into ; over
in plaats van	instead of
inchecken	check in *(at airport)*
inclusief	included
indigestie, de	indigestion
inenting, de	injection
informatie, de	information
informatiekantoor, het	information office
ingang, de	entrance ; way in
inkt, de	ink
inktvis, de	octopus ; squid
inlichtingen	enquiries
inpakken	wrap
inpakpapier, het	wrapping paper
insect, het	insect
insectenbeet, de	insect bite
insectenbestrijdings- middel, het	insect repellent
instapkaart, de	boarding card
instappen	to get in *(vehicle)*
instructeur, de	instructor
insuline, de	insulin
interessant	interesting
Intercity, de	intercity train
internationaal	international
interview, het	interview
introduceren	to introduce

intypen	to key in
invalide	disabled
invullen	to fill in *(form)*
inwisselen	to change *(money)* ; to cash *(cheque)*
is	is
Italiaans	Italian
Italië	Italy
ivoor, het	ivory

ja	yes
ja, alstublieft/graag	yes, please
ja	yes
jaar, het	year
jacht, het	yacht
jaloers	jealous
jam, de	jam *(food)*
januari	January
Japan	Japan
Japans	Japanese
jas, de	coat
jashanger, de	coat hanger
jasje, het	jacket
jazz	jazz
je	you *(sing. with friends)*
jeans, de	jeans
jenever, de	Dutch gin
jeugdherberg, de	youth hostel
jeuk, de	itch
jij	you *(sing. with friends)*
jol, de	dinghy
jong	young

jongen, de	**boy**
joods	**Jewish**
journalist, de	**journalist**
juli	**July**
jullie	**you** (plural with friends)
juni	**June**
jurk, de	**dress**
juwelen, de	**jewellery**
juwelier, de	**jeweller's**
kaal	**bald** (person)
kaart, de	**card ; map** (of region)
kaartje, het	**ticket**
kaartverkoop, de	**ticket sales, box office**
kaas, de	**cheese**
kachel, de	**heater**
kade, de	**quay**
kalfsvlees, het	**veal**
kalkoen, de	**turkey**
kalm	**calm**
kam, de	**comb**
kamer, de	**room** (in house, hotel)
kamerbediening, de	**room service**
kamermeisje, het	**maid** (in hotel)
kammossel, de	**scallop**
kamp, het	**camp**
kampeerauto, de	**camper** (car)
kan ik...?	**can I ...? ; may I ...?**
kanaal, het	**canal**
kano, de	**canoe**
kanoën	**canoeing**
kans, de	**chance**

kantoor, het	office
kapel, de	chapel
kapot	broken down *(machine, etc.)*
kapper, de	barber's ; hairdresser
karaf, de	carafe
karbonade, de	chop *(meat)*
kassa, de	cash desk ; till
kassabon, de	receipt
kassier, de	cashier *(male)*
kassière, de	cashier *(female)*
kast, de	cupboard
kastanje, de	chestnut
kasteel, het	castle
kat, de	cat
kater, de	hangover
kathedraal, de	cathedral
katholiek	Catholic
katje, het	kitten
katoen, het	cotton
kauwgom, de	chewing gum
keel, de	throat
keeltablet, het	throat lozenge
kennel, de	kennel
kennen	to know ; to be acquainted with
kennis, de	knowledge ; acquaintance
keren	to turn
kerk, de	church
kermis, de	fair *(funfair)*
kers, de	cherry
Kerstsmis	Christmas
ketting, de	chain
keuken, de	kitchen

kies, de	**tooth** *(back)*
kiespijn, de	**toothache**
kiezel, de	**pebble**
kijken (naar)	**to watch ; to look at**
kilo, de	**kilo**
kilometer, de	**kilometre**
kind, het	**child**
kinderbedje, het	**cot**
kinderen, de	**children** *(infants)*
kinderstoel, de	**high chair**
kiosk, de	**kiosk**
kip, de	**chicken**
klaar	**ready ; finished**
klaarmaken	**to prepare** *(incl. food)* **; to get ready**
klacht, de	**complaint**
klagen	**to complain**
klant, de	**client ; customer**
kleden	**to dress** *(get dressed)*
kleedkamer, de	**changing room** *(sport)*
kleerhanger, de	**clothes peg**
kleermaker, de	**tailor's**
klein	**little ; small**
kleiner	**smaller**
kleingeld, het	**change** *(money)* **; coins**
kleren, de	**clothes**
kleur, de	**colour**
kleuterschool, de	**nursery school**
klimmen	**to climb**
klok, de	**clock**
klompen, de	**clogs**
klooster, het	**monastery**
kloppen	**to knock ; knock** *(sign)*

Dutch	English
knie, de	knee
knijper, de	peg *(for clothes)*
knippen	to cut
knoflook, de	garlic
knolraap, de	turnip
knoop, de	button ; knot
koe, de	cow
koekepan, de	frying pan
koekje, het	biscuit
koel	cool
koelkast, de	fridge
koers, de	rate
koffer, de	case ; suitcase
koffie, de	coffee
koffie met melk	white coffee
koffie zonder caffeïne	decaffeinated coffee
kok, de	cook
koken	to boil ; to cook
kokosnoot, de	coconut
komen	to come
kom binnen!	come in!
komkommer, de	cucumber
konijn, het	rabbit
koning, de	king
koningin, de	queen
koninklijk	royal
kooktoestel, het	cooker
kool, de	cabbage
koorts, de	fever
kop, de	cup ; head *(of animal)*
kopen	to buy
kopie, de	copy
kopiëren	to copy
kort	short ; brief

korte broek, de	shorts
korting, de	reduction
kostbaar	valuable
kostbaarheden, de	valuables
kosten	to cost
kosten, de	charge (cost)
kostuum, het	suit
koud	cold
kousen, de	stockings
kraan, de	tap
krab, de	crab
krant, de	newspaper
kreeft, de	lobster
krent, de	currant
krijgen	to get ; to receive
krik, de	jack (for car)
kruid, het	herb
kruidenier, de	grocer's
kruidnagel, de	clove
kruik, de	jug
kruising, de	junction (road)
kruispunt, het	crossroads
kunnen	to be able
kunstgebit, het	dentures
kurketrekker, de	corkscrew
kus, de	kiss
kussen	to kiss
kussen, het	pillow
kussensloop, het	pillowcase
kust, de	coast ; seaside
kustwacht, de	coastguard
kwal, de	jellyfish
kwaliteit, de	quality

laag	low ; shallow
laan, de	lane
laars, de	boot
laat	late
ladder, de	ladder
laken, het	sheet *(for bed)*
lam, het	lamb
lamp, de	lamp
land, het	country ; nation ; land
lang	long ; tall ; large
langzaam	slow ; slowly
later	later
lawaai, het	noise
laxeermiddel, het	laxative
leeftijd, de	age
leeg	empty
leer, het	leather
legende, de	legend
leiden	to guide
leider, de	leader
lek, het	leak *(of gas, liquid, tyre, in roof)*
lenen	to lend ; to borrow
lengte, de	length
lens, de	lens *(photographic)*
lente, de	spring *(season)*
lepel, de	spoon
leraar, de	teacher *(male)*
lerares, de	teacher *(female)*
leren	to learn ; to teach
les, de	lesson
letter, de	letter *(of alphabet)*
leuk	nice ; funny *(amusing)*
leunstoel, de	armchair

leven	**to live**
leven, het	**life**
lever, de	**liver**
lezen	**to read**
licht	**light**
lichtblauw	**light blue**
lid, het	**member** (of club, etc.)
lied, het	**song**
lief	**lovely**
liefde, de	**love**
liegen	**to lie**
lieve	**dear**
lift, de	**lift**
liften	**hitchhike**
liggen	**to lie down**
lijfwacht, de	**lifeguard**
lijken	**to seem**
lijm, de	**glue**
lijn, de	**line**
lijnvlucht, de	**scheduled flight**
lijst, de	**list**
likeur, de	**liqueur**
limoen, de	**lime** (fruit)
limonade, de	**lemonade**
liniaal, de	**ruler** (measuring)
links	**left**
linksaf gaan	**turn left**
lippenstift, de	**lipstick**
lippenzalf, de	**lip salve**
liter	**litre**
loge, de	**box** (in theatre)
lokale	**local** (wine, speciality)
loket, het	**window** (ticket office) ; **counter**

lolly, de	lollipop
Londen	London
loodgieter, de	plumber
loodvrije benzine, de	unleaded petrol
loon, het	wage
lopen	to walk
losmaken	to unfasten
losschroeven	to unscrew
lotion, de	lotion
luchtdruk, de	tyre pressure
luchtmatras, de	air-mattress
luchtpost, de	air mail
luchtvaartmaatschappij, de	airline
lucifers, de	matches
lui	lazy
luid	loud
luier, de	nappy
luik, het	shutter *(on window)*
luisteren	to listen to
lunch, de	lunch
lunchpakket, het	packed lunch
luxe, de	luxury
maag, de	stomach
maaltijd, de	meal
maan, de	moon
maand, de	month
maandverband, het	sanitary towels
maar	but
maart	March
maat, de	size
macaroni, de	macaroni

machine, de	**machine**
mager	**skimmed** (milk, etc.)
make-up, de	**make-up**
maken	**to make** (generally)
makreel, de	**mackerel**
man, de	**man**
manager, de	**manager**
mand, de	**basket**
manier, de	**way** (manner)
mannelijk	**male**
mannen, de	**men**
margarine, de	**margarine**
marine blauw	**navy blue**
markt, de	**market**
marmelade, de	**marmalade**
marmer, het	**marble**
marsepein, de	**marzipan**
mast, de	**mast**
materiaal, het	**material**
mayonaise, de	**mayonnaise**
mazelen, de	**measles**
mechanicien, de	**engineer** (car)
mechanisch	**mechanic**
medicijn, het	**medicine**
meenemen	**to take out ; to take along**
meer	**more**
meer, het	**lake**
meeste	**most**
mei	**May**
meisje, het	**girl**
meisjesnaam, de	**maiden name**
mejuffrouw	**Miss**

melk, de	milk
meloen, de	melon
mengen	to mix
mengsel, het	mixture
mening, de	opinion
mens, de	human being
mensheid, de	mankind
menstruatie, de	period (menstruation)
menu, het	menu
merk, het	brand (of cigarettes, etc.)
mes, het	knife
mesje, het	blade (shaving)
met	with
metalen, de	metal
meten	to measure
meter	metre
meter, de	meter
metro, de	underground (metro)
meubelen, de	furniture
mevrouw (mevr.)	Mrs
middag, de	afternoon
middel, de	waist
middelen, de	means
midden	middle ; medium
middernacht	midnight
migraine, de	migraine
mijl, de	mile
mijnheer	Mr ; Sir ; Mister
miljoen	million
milkshake, de	milkshake
millimeter	millimetre
minder	less

mineraalwater, het	mineral water
minimum, het	minimum
minst	least
minuut, de	minute
mis, de	mass *(in church)*
missen	miss *(train, etc.)*
mist, de	fog
mistig	foggy
misverstand, het	misunderstanding
modder, de	mud
modern	modern
modieus	fashionable
moe	tired
moeder, de	mother
moeilijk	difficult
moeilijkheden, de	trouble
moer, de	nut *(for bolt)*
moersleutel, de	spanner
mogelijk	possible
molen, de	mill ; windmill
moment, het	moment
mond, de	mouth
monster, het	sample
monument, het	monument
mooi	beautiful ; fine ; pretty
morgen	tomorrow
morgen, de	morning
morgenavond	tomorrow evening
morgenmiddag	tomorrow afternoon
morgenochtend	tomorrow morning
mossel, de	mussel
mosterd, de	mustard
mot, de	moth *(clothes)*
motor, de	engine ; motor

motorboot, de	**motor boat**
motorfiets, de	**motor cycle**
mousserend	**fizzy**
muis, de	**mouse**
munt, de	**coin ; mint** *(herb)*
muntgeld, het	**coins**
museum, het	**museum**
muskiet, de	**mosquito**
muur, de	**wall** *(outside)*
muziek, de	**music**
na	**after**
naakt	**naked ; nude**
naald, de	**needle**
naam, de	**name**
naar beneden gaan	**to go down** *(stairs)*
naar	**to**
naast	**beside**
nacht, de	**night**
nachtclub, de	**night club**
nachtjapon, de	**nightdress**
nagel, de	**nail** *(fingernail)*
nagerecht, het	**dessert**
najaar, het	**autumn**
namaak	**fake**
nat	**wet**
natte verf	**wet paint**
nationaliteit, de	**nationality**
nauw	**narrow**
Nederland	**Netherlands, the**
Nederlander, de	**Dutchman**
Nederlands	**Dutch**

Nederlandse, de	Dutch woman
nee	no
neef, de	cousin (male) ; nephew
negatief, het	negative (photography)
nek, de	neck
nemen	to catch (bus, etc.) ; to take
nest, het	nest
netnummer, het	dialling code
neus, de	nose
nicht, de	cousin (female) ; niece
niemand	nobody
nieren, de	kidneys
niet	not
niets	nothing
nieuw	new
Nieuw Zeeland	New Zealand
Nieuwjaar	New Year
nieuws, het	news
nodig	necessary
nog	still adv ; yet
noodgeval, het	emergency
nooduitgang, de	emergency exit
nooit	never
noord	north
Noord-Ierland	Northern Ireland
nootmuskaat, de	nutmeg
november	November
nu	now
nuchter	sober
nul	zero
nummer, het	number
nummerbord, het	number plate (on car)
nuttig	useful

ober, de	waiter
oberkelner, de	head waiter
oefenboek, het	exercise book
oester, de	oyster
of	or
ogenblik, het	moment
o.k.	OK *(agreed)* ; good ; well
oktober	October
olie, de	oil
oliefilter, het	oil filter
olienoot, de	peanut
olijfolie, de	olive oil
olijven, de	olives
omelet, de	omelette
omgeven door	surrounded by
omleiding, de	bypass
omverrijden	knock down *(car)*
omweg, de	detour
oncomfortabel	uncomfortable
onder	below ; under
onderbreking, de	stopover
onderbroek, de	knickers ; underpants
onderdak, het	accommodation
onderdeel, het	item
onderdoorgang, de	underpass
ondergoed, het	underwear
ondersteboven	upside down
ondertekenen	to sign
oneven	odd
ongeluk, het	accident ; crash ; bad luck
ongelukkig	unhappy
ongetrouwd	single *(unmarried)*
ongeveer	approximately

onmiddellijk	immediately
onmogelijk	impossible
ons (onze)	our
ons, het	Dutch ounce ; 100 g
ontbijt, het	breakfast
ontdooien	to defrost
ontmoeten	to meet
ontmoeting, de	meeting
ontsmettingsmiddel, het	disinfectant
ontsteking, de	ignition
ontwikkelen	develop
onweer, het	lightning
onweersbui, de	thunderstorm
oog, het	eye
ooglid, het	eyelash
ook	also ; too
oom, de	uncle
oor, het	ear
oorbellen, de	earrings
oorlog, de	war
oorpijn, de	earache
oost	east
op	up ; on ; above
opbellen	to phone ; to ring
opeens	suddenly
open	open
openbaar	public
opendraaien	to open (tap)
openen	to open
opera, de	opera
opgewonden	excited
oppas, de	babysitter
oppassen	to mind ; to be careful

oproepen	to call
opschieten	to hurry up
optillen	to lift *(weight)*
opwindend	exciting
oranje	orange *(colour)*
organiseren	to organize
oud	old
ouders, de	parents
oven, de	oven
over	in ; over ; about *(relating to)*
overhemd, het	shirt
overjas, de	overcoat
overmorgen	the day after tomorrow
overtreding, de	offence *(crime)*
overweg, de	level crossing
p.a.	care of ; c/o
paar, het	pair ; couple *(2 people)*
paard, het	horse
paars	purple
pad, het	path
pak, het	pack *(luggage)* ; suit
pakken	to take ; to grab ; to pack
pak maar	just take it
pakje, het	packet ; parcel
pakpapier, het	wrapping paper
paleis, het	palace
paling, de	eel
pan, de	pan
pannekoek, de	pancake
panties, de	tights
papier, het	paper

paprika, de	**pepper** (vegetable)
paraffine, de	**paraffin**
paraplu, de	**umbrella**
pardon!	**excuse me!**
pardon?	**pardon?**
parfum, het	**perfume**
park, het	**park**
parkeerplaats, de	**car park ; parking space**
parkeerschijf, de	**parking disk**
parkeren	**to park**
Pasen	**Easter**
paskamer, de	**changing room** (shop)
paspoortcontrole, de	**passport control**
paspoort, het	**passport**
passagier, de	**passenger**
passen	**to fit** (clothes)
pasta, de	**pasta**
pastei, de	**pastry** (meat pie)
patat, de	**chips**
paté, de	**pâté**
pauze, de	**interval** (theatre, etc.)
peen, de	**carrot**
peer, de	**pear**
pen, de	**pen**
penicilline, de	**penicillin**
pension, het	**boarding house ; guesthouse**
peper, de	**pepper** (spice)
pepermuntje, het	**peppermint** (sweet)
per	**by ; per**
perfect	**perfect**
permanent, het	**perm**
perron, het	**platform** (train)
persoon, de	**person**

perzik, de	peach
peterselie, de	parsley
picknick, de	picnic
pijn, de	pain ; ache
pijnlijk	painful
pijnstiller, de	painkiller
pijp, de	pipe (smoker's)
pikant	spicy
pil, de	pill
pils	pilsner ; lager
pinchet, het	tweezers
pinda, de	peanut
plaat, de	record (music)
plak, de	slice (of ham)
plakband, het	adhesive tape ; Sellotape®
plastic	plastic
plat	flat ; level
plattegrond, de	map ; plan
platteland, het	countryside (not town)
plein, het	square (in town)
pleister, de	plaster ; sticking plaster
poederkoffie, de	instant coffee
poedermelk, de	powdered milk
politie, de	police
politiebureau, het	police station
pond, het Britse	pound (money)
pond, het	Dutch pound (weight) ; 0.5 k
pont, de	ferry
pop, de	doll
popmuziek, de	pop music
port, de	port (wine)
portefeuille, de	wallet
portemonnaie, de	purse

portier, de	**porter**
portret, het	**portrait**
Portugal	**Portugal**
Portugees	**Portuguese**
postbus	**PO Box**
postcode, de	**postcode**
posten	**to post**
postkantoor, het	**post office**
postzegel, de	**stamp** *(postage)*
pot, de	**jar** *(container)* ; **pot** *(for cooking)*
potlood, het	**pencil**
praten	**to talk**
precies	**exact**
prefereren	**to prefer**
prei, de	**leek**
prestatie, de	**performance**
priester, de	**priest**
prijs, de	**price** ; **prize**
prijslijst, de	**price list**
prins, de	**prince**
prinses, de	**princess**
privé	**private**
proberen	**to try** *(attempt)*
probleem, het	**problem**
producent, de	**producer** *(TV, film)*
proeven	**to taste**
programma, het	**programme**
proost!	**cheers!**
protestant	**Protestant**
pruim, de	**plum** ; **prune**
pudding, de	**pudding**
pullover, de	**pullover**
pyjama, de	**pyjamas**

raam, het	**window**
raar	**strange ; silly**
rabarber, de	**rhubarb**
radijsjes, de	**radishes**
radio, de	**radio**
raken	**to hit**
ras, het	**race**
rat, de	**rat**
rauw	**raw**
realiseren	**to realise**
recent	**recent**
recentelijk	**recently**
recept, het	**prescription ; recipe**
receptie, de	**reception** (desk)
recht	**straight**
rechtdoor	**straight on**
rechts	**right** (side)
rechtsaf gaan	**turn right**
rechtstreeks	**direct** (train, etc.)
redden	**to save**
reddingsboot, de	**lifeboat**
reddingsvest, het	**life jacket**
reden, de	**reason**
regelen	**to arrange**
regen, de	**rain**
regenjas, de	**raincoat**
regenkleding, de	**rainclothes**
registreren	**to register** (at hotel)
reis, de	**journey ; trip**
reisbureau, het	**travel agent**
reisgids, de	**guidebook**
reizen	**to travel**
rekenen	**to charge** (meney)

rekening, de	bill ; invoice
rekenmachine, de	calculator
relatie, de	relation *(family)*
relaxen	to relax
rem, de	brake
remvloeistof, de	brake fluid
reparatiewagen, de	breakdown van
repareren	to repair
reserve	reserve ; spare
reserveren	to book ; to reserve
reservering, de	booking
reiskosten, de	fare
restaurant, het	restaurant
restauratie, de	buffet
restauratiewagen, de	buffet car
retour, het	return ticket
reuk, de	smell
reumatiek, de	arthritis
riem, de	belt
rietje, het	straw *(for drinking)*
rij, de	line ; row ; queue
rijbewijs, het	driving licence
rijden	to drive ; to ride
rijk	rich *(person, etc.)*
rijomstandigheden, de	road conditions
rijp	ripe
rijst, de	rice
rijstrook, de	carriage *(of motorway)*
rijtuig, het	carriage *(train)*
ring, de	ring *(wedding)*
riolering, de	drains *(sewage system)*
ritssluiting, de	zip
rivier, de	river

Dutch	English
rode bes, de	redcurrant
rode biet, de	beetroot
rode hond, de	German measles
roeiboot, de	rowing boat
roeien	to row (boat)
roeiriem, de	oar
roepen	to call (shout)
roer, het	rudder
roereieren, de	scrambled eggs
roestig	rusty
roggebrood, het	rye bread
roken	to smoke
rolstoel, de	pushchair ; wheelchair
roltrap, de	escalator
roman, de	novel
rond	round (shape)
rondgang, de	guided tour
rondkijken	to browse
rondleiding, de	guided tour (in museum, etc.)
röntgenstralen, de	X-rays
rood	red
rook, de	smoke
room, de	cream (on milk)
roos, de	rose
roosteren	to roast
rose	pink
rosé	rosé (wine)
rot	rotten (fruit, etc.)
rotonde, de	roundabout (traffic)
route, de	route
rozijn, de	raisin
rubber	rubber (material)
rubberboot, de	dinghy (rubber)

Dutch	English
rug, de	**back** (of body)
rugzak, de	**backpack ; rucksack**
ruiken	**to smell**
ruimte, de	**space**
ruïne, de	**ruins**
rum, de	**rum**
rundvlees, het	**beef**
rust, de	**rest** (repose)
rusten	**to rest**
ruw	**rough** (sea)
ruzie, de	**quarrel**
salade, de	**salad**
samen	**together**
sandalen, de	**sandals**
sandwich, de	**sandwich**
sap, het	**juice**
sardine, de	**sardine**
sauna, de	**sauna**
saus, de	**dressing** (for food) **; sauce**
schaaldieren, de	**shellfish**
schaap, het	**sheep**
schaar, de	**scissors**
schaatsen	**skating**
schaatsen, de	**skates**
schade, de	**damage**
schaduw, de	**shade**
schakelaar, de	**switch**
schapevlees, het	**mutton**
scheercrème, de	**shaving cream**
scheermes, het	**razor**
scheermesjes, de	**razor blades**

schenken	**to pour**
scheren	**to shave**
scheur, de	**tear** (in material)
schieten	**to shoot**
schikken	**to suit**
schilderij, het	**painting**
schillen	**to peel** (fruit)
schip, het	**ship**
schoen, de	**shoe**
schoenpoetsmiddel, het	**polish** (for shoes)
schoenveters, de	**laces** (of shoe)
schok, de	**shock**
schokdemper, de	**shock absorber**
schommel, de	**swing** (children's)
school, de	**school**
schoon	**clean**
schoonheidsmiddelen, de	**cosmetics**
schoonmaakmiddel, het	**cleansing material**
schoonmaken	**to clean**
schoonmoeder, de	**mother-in-law**
schoonvader, de	**father-in-law**
schop, de	**spade**
schoppen	**to kick**
schotel, de	**saucer**
Schotland	**Scotland**
Schots	**Scottish**
schreeuwen	**to shout**
schrijfpapier, het	**writing paper**
schrijfwarenhandel, de	**stationer's**
schrijven	**to write**
schroef, de	**screw**
schroevendraaier, de	**screwdriver**
schuimgebak, het	**meringue**

schuld	**fault, guilt**
schutting, de	**fence**
score, de	**score**
scoren	**to score** (goal)
seizoenkaart, de	**season ticket**
selderie, de	**celery**
september	**September**
serie, de	**series**
serieus	**serious** (person)
serveerster, de	**waitress**
servet, het	**napkin**
shampoo, de	**shampoo**
shandy, het	**shandy**
sherry, de	**sherry**
shirt, het	**jersey** (football)
show, de	**show**
sigaar, de	**cigar**
sigarenwinkel, de	**tobacconist's**
sigaret, de	**cigarette**
simpel	**simple**
sinaasappel, de	**orange**
sinaasappelsap, het	**orange juice** (fresh)
sjaal, de	**scarf**
sla, de	**lettuce**
slaapkamer, de	**bedroom**
slaappil, de	**sleeping pill**
slaapwagen, de	**couchette ; sleeper** (on train)
slaapzak, de	**sleeping bag**
slager, de	**butcher's**
slang, de	**hose**
slap	**weak**
slapen	**to sleep**
slecht	**bad** (weather, news)

slechter	worse
slechts	only
slee, de	sledge
sleepkabel, de	tow rope
slepen	to tow
sleutel, de	key
sleutelhanger, de	key-ring
slijter, de	off-license shop
slikken	to swallow
slipper, de	slipper
slot, het	lock (on door, box)
sluiten	to shut
smaak, de	flavour ; taste
smaken	to taste (good or bad)
smelten	to melt
snackbar, de	snack bar ; chip shop
snee, de	cut ; slice (of bread)
sneeuw, de	snow
sneeuwen	snowing
snel	fast
snelheid, de	speed
snelheidslimiet, de	speed limit
sneltrein, de	fast train ; express train
snijbonen, de	french beans
snijden	to cut
snoep, het	sweets
snor, de	moustache
snorkel, de	snorkel
sober	sober
soda, het	soda
soep, de	soup
sokken, de	socks
soms	sometimes

Dutch	English
soort, het	**kind** (sort, type)
sorry	**sorry**
souvenir, het	**souvenir**
Spaanse peper, de	**chilli**
sparen	**to save** (money)
speciaal	**special**
specialiteit, de	**speciality**
speelgoed, het	**toy**
speelkamer, de	**playroom**
speen, de	**teat ; dummy** (for baby)
spek, het	**bacon**
spel, het	**game ; play**
speld, de	**pin**
spellen	**to spell**
spiegel, de	**mirror**
spier, de	**muscle**
spijker, de	**nail** (metal)
spinazie, de	**spinach**
spitsuur, het	**rush hour**
splitsing, de	**junction** (in road)
spoel, de	**reel**
spons, de	**sponge**
spoor, het	**platform** (train)
spoorweg, de	**railway**
sport, de	**sport**
sprankelend	**sparkling**
spreken	**to speak**
springen	**to jump**
spruiten, de	**Brussels sprouts**
spuwen	**to spit**
squash	**squash** (game)
staart, de	**tail**
stad, de	**city ; town**

stadhuis, het	**town hall**
staking, de	**strike**
stalles, de	**stalls** (theatre)
starten	**to start** (car)
startkabel, de	**jump leads**
station, het	**station** (railway, bus)
steelpan, de	**saucepan**
steen, de	**stone**
steken	**to sting**
stekker, de	**plug** (electrical)
stem, de	**voice**
ster, de	**star**
sterk	**strong**
sterke drank	**spirits** (drink)
steward, de	**steward** (on plane)
stewardess, de	**stewardess** (on plane)
stier, de	**bull**
stijl	**style ; steep**
stil	**silent ; quiet** (place)
stilte, de	**silence**
stoel, de	**chair**
stoep, de	**pavement**
stof, de	**fabric ; material** (cloth)
stof, het	**dust**
stofzuiger, de	**vacuum cleaner**
stomerij, de	**dry-cleaner's**
stoofpot, de	**stew**
stop	**stop**
stop, de	**stopper** (for sink)
stoptrein, de	**slow train**
storm, de	**storm**
straat, de	**street**
strand, het	**beach**

streng verboden...	**strictly forbidden...** (sign)
strijken	**to iron**
strijkijzer, het	**iron** (for clothes)
strippenkaart, de	**public transport ticket** (for several trips)
stropdas, de	**tie**
student, de	**student**
stug	**tough** (meat)
stuk	**broken**
stuk, het	**piece ; play** (theatre)
sturen	**to send**
succes, het	**success**
suède, het	**suede**
suiker, de	**sugar**
suikerziekte, de	**diabetes**
supermarkt, de	**supermarket**
supporter, de	**fan** (football)
surfplank, de	**surfboard**
s.v.p.	**please** (abbreviation)
synagoge, de	**synagogue**
T-shirt, het	**teeshirt**
taal, de	**language**
taart, de	**cake**
tabak, de	**tobacco**
tablet, het	**tablet**
tafel, de	**table**
tafellaken, het	**tablecloth**
tafelkleed, het	**tablecloth**
tafelwijn, de	**table wine**
talk, de	**talc**
tam	**tame**